P9-DNR-029

DISCARD

LOWER CLASS

The Author at Age Twenty-seven.

LOWER CLASS

By

GEORGE YOUELL

Illustrations by Anton Otto Fischer

1938

GEORGE YOUELL

Seattle, Washington

COPYRIGHT 1938 BY
GEORGE YOUELL

Printed and bound in the United States of America by
The CAXTON PRINTERS, Ltd.
Caldwell, Idaho
50110

FOREWORD

THIS BOOK, like *Cranford, Old Chester Tales,* and *The Bible in Spain,* gives pleasure to all kinds of readers. For it is a frank and detailed narration of facts about the lives of a little-known section of our Anglo-Saxon deep-sea fishermen by one who knows what he writes about from personal experience, and who, having won out to affluence, has the unusual gift of being willing to tell his own story of rising from what we call the "lower class," and has the wit to do it well. It is now recognized even in England that a ranker can become an officer in any calling in life, and that claim to gentility rests on truer foundations than silver spoons or recorded genealogies; powerful in character building as those factors may be.

But still some of the old snobbery exists, the class divisions being oddly enough as rigidly maintained among rich and poor.

Having shared the lives of my fellowmen of many classes, those of fishermen especially, and having sailed with North Sea trawlers many, many times, I can vouch for the fact that this book underestimates, if anything, the physical hardship of their lives, and testify that they are possibly for that very reason a more happy, more lovable and more worthwhile lot of human beings than many in other classes quite differently labeled. Seeing that Peter and Andrew, James and John were selected as bosom companions and friends by the Wisest of Men, and also that these "lower class" men did turn the world upside down, there is no need to defend this deduction of experience. There was no representative of Wall Street, no bank or college president, nor any proportion of scientific experts among the men who saved England from the Spaniards, who sailed on the *Mayflower* to the new world, or in the little company of men who laid their lives down for the Christian philosophy to which our western civilization owes so much, if not all.

In our family, we read this book aloud, and enjoyed it thoroughly. It gives a truer yet as interesting a picture of the class it describes than W. W. Jacobs or P. G. Wodehouse do of those they write of, and it is lightened throughout by a very keen sense of humour.

I heartily commend anyone to give time to this excellent little volume.

WILFRED T. GRENFELL.

LIST OF ILLUSTRATIONS

LOWER CLASS

I was born in 1868 in a small village in that part of England known as East Anglia. The two counties of Norfolk and Suffolk comprising East Anglia are off the route of the average tourist. They contain many places and features of historic interest, but as England is everywhere so well supplied with historical attractions, why, argues the tourist, should he leave the beaten path to see a few additional cathedrals, abbeys, and castles when such sights are inescapable on any route? East Anglia is a rich agricultural country, but work horses, cows, and pigs are not often regarded as special attractions. The seaports of Yarmouth and Lowestoft were important centers of trade at the time when I was privileged to know them well, but the trade was mainly that of fishing or fish curing, a somewhat specialized business. Those who were engaged in this trade could be easily identified, in spite of the hottest of baths and a change from the skin out. The smell of fish is most tenacious. A Frenchman has no objection to the smell of garlic; having never been out of reach of the odor, he does not know it exists. Tourists, however, or at least those of the "better class," did not consider our fishing ports as the ultimate in seaside resorts, mainly on account of the smell of fish—which really should have been considered as an added attraction with no additional cost. The natives who had never drawn a breath of air wholly untempered with the captivating smell of fish could not sense the reason for their criticism. Certainly if one were allowed to select his birthplace, he could find no spot on earth more favorable for that great adventure than the wonderful country of East Anglia.

My parents were poor people, a term which no one born or reared in the United States of America can ever fully understand. Most men are proud of their parents even though they may entertain well-founded misgivings as to any reason why the sentiment should be mutual. I am very proud of mine. They were a wonderful couple who retained their love and respect for each other long past their golden wedding anniversary and to the journey's end. Although they spent a large part of their lives in what would be considered the direst poverty, as judged by the American standard, they thought they were living lives of comparative affluence.

My mother gave birth to twelve children. She never attended a birth control lecture in her life and would have considered literature on the subject, had there been any extant at the time, as the teaching of the devil. Three of the children died in infancy, but though she still had nine to care for, my mother never appeared to feel that her family was burdensome. She was proud of the fact that she had so many fine healthy children, and her days were full of gratitude for her many blessings. When she tucked us in at night, three or four in a bed, she would remind us of how much we had to be thankful for. We had had our suppers, we were in warm beds; many children were supperless, and some had no beds. As everything is a matter of comparison, we could readily agree with Mother that our lot was indeed an envious one. She would speak to us of our father and of how proud we should be of him. He was such an exceptional man who brought all of his earnings—which as a teamster on a farm did not average more than fifteen shillings a week—to the care of his family, and he did not spend his money for beer as many did at the village inn.

On Sundays we, or at least a group of us, were taken to church. My parents adhered to the Church of England; they had never become Dissenters and gone over to the Methodists. Because of family cares, it was not often that my mother was able to accompany us in person although I am sure she did so in spirit. She observed the day, however, as fully as possible at home. No cooking was done on Sunday, and a restraining influence which we understood but failed to appreciate was held over us children on that day. The boys were not allowed to whistle, and we were not allowed to romp as our abundant health and usually high spirits prompted us to do, but during the rest of the week we were allowed to burn up energy with utter recklessness. On Sunday evenings, such of us as were able to read, read in turn verses from a chapter in the Bible.

We did not see much of our father. He left very early in the morning to feed the horses so they would be in readiness for the day's work. There were several horses on the farm where my father worked, but he fed and cared for all of them, although other men, receiving slightly less wages on account of their shorter working hours, worked some of the horses.

Previous to her marriage my mother had been a dairymaid, and of this experience she was very proud. Although both of my parents were members of large families, they never mentioned the fact that any relative had ever been above their own rank of teamster and dairymaid.

They were good Christians, but quiet ones. This was probably the reason why they preferred the Episcopal to the more demonstrative Methodist service. My father often hummed Gospel songs of which he appeared to know many. It never occurred to either of them that a lie could be substituted for the truth. They interpreted the Ten Commandments literally and did not covet their neighbor's goods. Some may conclude that at the time and under the conditions which they lived their paths were not beset with the temptations of the present day. But they had the same devil or devils to contend with that make the ways of the righteous so difficult at the present time. Mother made all commitments with the qualification, "God willing."

It is a poor citizen of any country, be he natural or adopted, who is not proud of the land of his birth. I am proud of the fact that I was born in East Anglia. My parentage, the land of my birth, and the conditions of life into which I was born were all favorable to a life of maximum usefulness. I have never justified my fine parentage, my many inherited advantages, the advice and care given by my exceptional father and mother.

Revolutions are rare, and the aversion to change is deeply rooted in the average Englishman. Living conditions and habits of thought are now as they were sixty or one hundred and sixty years ago and, according to my observation, society continues as I found it at the time of my birth, rather loosely organized into several classes—royalty naturally being held in the highest esteem. This was followed by the nobility, then the upper class or gentry, upper middle class, lower middle class, lower class, and the submerged class. The greater portion of the entire population were members of the lower class, but lower middle class and the submerged class were quite sizeable in numbers. Tramps, permanent residents of workhouses, ne'er-do-wells, criminals, and incompetents composed the submerged class. Very few of this latter class would be found in East Anglia. There the magistrates were the principal taxpayers and they made life extremely burdensome to those who sought to live at their expense. These local or magistrate courts were no doubt model institutions for the dispensation of justice, but the word "mercy" was not inscribed on their portals. As a result of this lack of sympathy on the part of the taxpayer magistrates, those who planned to live a life of ease at the expense of the community would locate in the towns and cities where the contact between the taxpayer and dependent was usually less intimate.

These class distinctions were quite easily maintained. It was rare that anyone moved more than ten miles from the place of his birth, and for the most part people died in the village where they were born. Everybody knew the antecedents of his neighbors, and no imaginable measure of thrift could materially change his financial status. A good-looking girl of the lower class might receive proposals from the males of classes higher than her own, but marriage would not be one of them. Nor could the most unattractive spinster of even the lower middle class be made to see that marriage to a laborer was preferable to permanent spinsterhood. Had she taken such an unwise step, she would have been ostracized by both classes. Her laborer mate's family would have refused to accept her, and something

(14)

more than marriage to one of its members is needed to persuade a properly established lower middle class family to accept a laborer into its fold. However, if a member of lower class insisted on becoming a lousy tramp or a confirmed criminal—poaching and just plain drunkenness were not regarded by lower class members as justifiably punishable offences—he could descend to the submerged class even though he might not be appreciated by his new associates. Hunting and fishing in any country are apparently man's inalienable rights. It is no doubt an hereditary instinct brought down from the days when men lived by hunting and fishing. American citizens are usually very law-abiding as to the observance of closed seasons on game and fish, but I am sure that if any law were ever passed giving one class of Americans the exclusive right to hunt or fish, that the law would be observed more by its violation than by its observance.

My parents were members of lower class and were as solidly entrenched as though the family had received its letters patent from William the Conqueror. My father, who had a somewhat restless disposition, occasionally expressed mild disapproval of the social order, but nothing could have induced him to accept social recognition from those who were commonly regarded as his betters. Father was a devoted reader of the Bible and as such he saw that society was not at that time ordered wholly on the teachings of the Book. Mother had no such misgivings. Victoria was Queen by Divine Appointment, and others held the rank or station they enjoyed on equally secure ground. What more could anyone desire than that they be able to maintain that station in life to which as the Church service expressed it, "It had pleased God to call them"? Certainly this was the philosophical view, for their chances of advancing to a higher social position were so exceedingly remote that they might have been regarded as wholly nonexistent. Both of my parents, however, were blessed with an abiding faith in a future reward, and their only immediate concern was for the needs of the day.

To be the child of lower class parents has many and great advantages: no inherent responsibilities, no overwhelming handicap of the achievements of predecessors, no family record to maintain, other than one for honesty. The fortunate individual who enters the world by this route finds himself beset with opportunities for adventure and self-improvement also, if he has any urge for its attainment. I was born with a spirit for mild adventure but unfortunately have never felt any craving for self-improvement. No other condition of birth can possibly offer so large an opportunity for a life of enjoyment; there was nothing to avoid but a plunge to the submerged class, and only unspeakable laziness or a total disregard for the rights of others could cause that to happen. It would no doubt be possible for a son of middle class parents to descend to the submerged class, but it is not conceivable that any child born to the upper class or nobility could do so. Family pride would prevent such a happening. They would be sent "abroad" and monthly remittances forwarded to them, which remittances would be so calculated that the recipient would never have enough money at one time to buy a ticket for home. There is no doubt but that these unpromising sons, when divested of the restraints of class distinctions, have often found in the land of their enforced adoption opportunities for useful and productive lives.

When I first saw myself in the mirror I was a chubby, curly, red-haired, and very well-nourished lad. By the time I was four years old I was ready to begin making observations. The world to me then appeared as a wonderful place; today it appears even more so. I was then, as I am now, quite well pleased with what the world has to offer. I was well fed and warmly clothed. I have continued all of my life to be well fed—frequently overfed—and warmly clothed, though in spite of all the clothes I owned, I have sometimes suffered from exposure to cold.

At age four no particular demands were made on me. An occasional short errand for my mother was the only interruption to a full day of play and the enjoyment of life to the full extent of my four-year-old capacity. Some of the results of my early observations were to the effect that we lived in a small brick cottage, the north one of a row of four which adjoined. The value of a sunny exposure was probably unknown to my parents. However, the windows were so very small that had the house enjoyed an all-day exposure to the sun, it is not likely that we should have been much benefited thereby. Being to that extent deprived of the sun's beneficial influence did not apparently seriously affect the family health. Neither could my parents have been justly accused of being "fresh air fiends," my mother having a peculiar horror of "night air." As we children played and sat on the hearth rug on the brick floor of the cottage, open doors would have subjected us to unnecessary drafts. The cottages each had a frontage of twelve or fourteen feet with gardens in the rear of the same width.

The rent of our cottage was two shillings a week. This was the maximum that could be afforded for rent. Most of the cottages were owned or controlled by the farmers or landowners. The collection of the

"We lived in a small brick cottage."

rentals was simplified by deducting the amount due each week from the wages which had been earned. Renting houses for two shillings a week, or two dollars a month, would not make a very strong appeal to the average American landlord. But American landlords may not always know all that there is to be known about renting houses. In England styles in dog kennels, pigstys and laborers' cottages have not changed perceptibly during the past five hundred years. What better investment would a conservative-minded person need than a row of cottages which paid a shilling on the pound annually for three or four hundred years? With brick walls and floors, and tiled roofs, the item of depreciation could be ignored, or at least left to the consideration of some far distant future generation. The interiors were whitewashed by, or at the expense of, the tenant. Whitewash is a most wholesome interior finish which requires but a minimum of skill for its application.

Adjoining us to the south lived the Snobeys, who were blessed, though they may have felt that they were cursed, with a large family of small children. These Snobey children were not a very sturdy crowd. They frequently had earache and other painful and annoying disorders. It was rumored—and no one has better opportunity to pick up rumors and gossip than has a four-year-old—that Mrs. Snobey was a woman with a past. If one judged by her appearance at that time, her "past" was a long way past and with the exercise of a little charity might have been forgotten. But so little of new experience came into the lives of our villagers that they were reluctant to part with or dismiss from their minds any item which would serve as a subject for gossip or discussion. It was stated that Snobey had met his wife when on shore leave while he was serving in the navy. If she was a fair sample of what the sailors met when they came on shore, the wonder is that they did not stay on their ships. However, Snobey had become infatuated with her and removed her from the sailor's welcoming committee by making her his wife. If he was no longer infatuated with her, it was at least known in the village that he was still insanely jealous, though most unnecessarily so, of what he regarded as her charms.

On the north we were bounded by the premises of Mr. Topping, or perhaps more correctly, "the Toppings." Mr. Topping was the village blacksmith, but there was also Mrs. Topping, Helen Topping, the daughter, and a son, Robert. Their premises consisted of a small garden and a patch of lawn about sixteen by sixteen. The house was on the farther side of the premises from our house and on a corner which was formed by a local road crossing the London highway or turnpike at this point. At the rear of the house and adjoining it was the blacksmith shop. As long as we continued to live in this location, I was fascinated by this family and its activities. We lived next door to the Toppings until I was six years of age—with the garden and lawn intervening they probably never felt that they lived next door to us—and during that time they furnished me with endless entertainment. It was my delight to stand in front of the door of the blacksmith shop—I was never allowed to set foot inside—and watch Mr. Topping fit a horse with a new set of shoes. By heating the shoe red hot and then applying it to the horse's hoof, he could determine where more paring was necessary. Horses' hoofs are not sensitive to heat, a fact of which the automobile-riding reader may not be aware. Mr. Topping also repaired broken farm machinery and farm implements. The Toppings were a gracious kindly family but in some shuffle of class lines they had been jolted out of their accustomed groove and had never definitely relocated themselves. They had become imbued with the idea that they were lower middle class. England was then known as the "land of the free," but this freedom did not mean that anyone should attempt to inject themselves into any social position to which they, and at least as far back as their great grandparents, had not been born. I think my father was disposed to grant the Toppings the social rating to which they aspired, for when I asked him why the Toppings never spoke to us as the Snobeys did—all too frequently—he replied that we were not in the Toppings' class. They lived suspended as it were between the two social divisions, and in spite of their kindly dispositions and general goodness of heart were rather cordially disliked by both sides. Their ambition to establish themselves as lower middle class members may perhaps be regarded as laudable, but apparently they might almost as well have striven to prove that they were of royal blood. If they ever succeeded in their ambition, it was after we left the neighborhood. The son, Robert, was absent at school most of the time, possibly learning the latest methods of horseshoeing, but during the summer holidays when Robert was at home the family carried on in fine lower middle class style. They had a pony and a tiny cart in which the parents rode facing the pony, while Helen and Robert sat with their backs to their parents and enjoyed a sort of rear platform view of the scenery.

Our village had two carpenters: Forman, who was recognized as a first-class artisan, and Bundy, who was considered a sort of hog-pen carpenter. Forman had a shop large enough to admit a farm wagon. He was the official coffinmaker when coffins were needed. Before commencing this delicate task of making a coffin he would visit the home of the deceased and carefully measure the corpse both as to length and width. It was usually the first time the subject had been measured for anything and was quite definitely the last time that any such measurements would be needed. Later he would call and screw down the lid of the coffin. Sometimes Bundy worked for Forman when the rush of work was unusually heavy. When he was thus employed he received three shillings a day as wages but furnished his own tools. While Mr. Bundy was not considered a first-class mechanic and no one entrusted him with the making of a coffin, still Mr. Bundy himself had confidence in his ability to make coffins and possibly as a rebuke to those who did not hold the same good opinion of his skill and to save his good-looking widow from Forman's extortions, he had made his own coffin and, preparatory to the time when it would be needed, it rested on two brackets high on the wall of his little workshop. On one of my infrequent visits to my birthplace, I learned that it was some sixty years after it was made—Mr. Bundy having almost rounded out a century—before Mr. Bundy's self-made coffin was needed and long after both Forman and the attractive Mrs. Bundy had passed on to where extortion is neither practiced or suffered. Styles in East Anglia change infrequently, and there is no doubt that Mr. Bundy's coffin when finally used was regarded as a quite recent masterpiece.

One morning Mr. Bundy appeared upon the Topping sixteen-by-sixteen lawn, and shortly afterwards a small load of lumber was delivered. My eyes were probably popping with excitement as to what was about to take place. Mr. Bundy proceeded with the deliberation the occasion demanded to construct a small, or rather, very small summer or teahouse. Had I been a witness to Noah laying the keel for his ark, I could not have been more impressed. This was the most wonderful piece of work that had ever been carried on under my observation. I watched construction almost to the exclusion of my meals. From sills to ridgepole I followed the work with unabated interest. Mr. Bundy was no doubt dealing direct with Mr. Topping in this matter, for the blacksmith was much too wide awake to allow Forman a middleman's profit on such a contract. Soon it was finished and painted white with green trimmings. The erection of a duplicate of Saint Paul's in the vicinity would not have interested me more. As it was built quite close to the road and with no hedge in the front of the garden, I had an indisputable right to a front position, if not to a front seat, to watch proceedings. To be really good lower middle class requires that one has a lawn, but the teahouse was almost an indication of upper middle class status. Apparently the Toppings were prepared to go to any extreme to show to one and all where they belonged in the social setup. As soon as the paint was dry, tea was served in the summer-house. Helen would appear at the door leading

"At age four none of my person was much above the ground."

from the house to the blacksmith shop and announce, "Papa, tea is served." "Papa" was distinctly a middle class affectation. Lower class fathers were never addressed as "Papa," although the term "Daddy" was occasionally used. "Father" was the customary term.

A high and quite thick privet hedge separated our tiny garden from that of the Toppings. To grownups this afforded a full measure of privacy, but nearer the ground the hedge was not so thick and at age four none of my person was much above the ground. While I had a clear view of the Topping premises from the road, I could often unseen and unsuspected get a much better view of what our neighbors were doing by looking through the hedge. Before leaving the shop, Mr. Topping would remove his leather apron, give the horse he was shoeing the relief of standing on all fours for awhile, wash his hands in the iron trough where the water was kept for cooling off the horseshoes after the final fitting and before they were nailed on permanently. He would then proceed to the summerhouse to drink tea. In all of East Anglia there was no man more poorly equipped for the rôle of afternoon tea drinker than he. A short, heavy-set, swarthy man with huge calloused hands, he was more in his element when shoeing a restless horse or swinging a sledge hammer than in drinking tea from a delicate little china cup. A quart of beer in a pewter mug would have been much more appropriate. But the biggest of men are easily led, or misled, by aspiring wives. This afternoon tea appeared to be the dividing line between lower class and lower middle class; not that the observance of the function would in itself alone establish the devotee. No, indeed—one could not bound over the social fences with such ease, but it was a function which was observed by lower middle class and even more closely observed by any who aspired ever to be relieved of lower class shackles.

The Toppings had but few intimates but they had one whom Mr. Topping greatly admired. This was a Mr. Everett who held a farm of about one hundred acres under lease. Usually such an activity would have given a man so engaged, or his family, the status of lower middle class, but Mr. Everett was comparatively a newcomer in the neighborhood and had never gone to much trouble to establish his family socially. Social standing requires the very close co-operation of all the family members, and Mrs. Everett could not alone carry out this responsibility. Mr. Everett appeared to like Mr. Topping. They drank beer together at the Red Lion, the village inn diagonally across the crossroads from the Topping residence and workshop. They always entered the "parlor," a room reserved for anyone above lower class who happened to call. In this room beer was served in glasses and not in mugs as in the barroom where the lower class congregated.

Served in this manner, beer was slightly more expensive, but Mr. Topping no doubt felt justified in incurring the additional expense or, by what required much more reasoning, convinced himself that he could take short measure in beer if it only helped toward the end that he—and his wife and daughter more particularly—had in mind.

A few houses down the road south from our house lived a widow named Alp, an elderly woman who meant nothing in my life, however, as she had no children with whom I could play. Occasionally the widow Alp had as a house guest a brother named Jackson who was by calling—as he had never achieved officer's rank it could hardly be considered as a profession—a sailor. Mr. Jackson was a quiet middle-aged man who, when on these visits, spent all day at the Red Lion. No one was particularly interested in him or the experiences which he was at all times anxious to relate. They knew nothing of the different countries that Jackson had visited and may sometimes have even doubted their existence. Jackson drank beer all day long and by night was usually mildly intoxicated but he would return in the morning and spend the day as he spent the one previous, drinking and talking to such as had time to listen to him. By contact with the villagers and in conversations with his sister, he was kept quite well informed on the slowly written history of the parish, and thus he learned of the friendship existing between the blacksmith and Mr. Everett. Stopping at the blacksmith shop one morning before he had had time to get drunk, he accosted the blacksmith with a "Good morning, Mr. Topping." Mr. Topping ignored the salutation. What were things coming to when this common sailor could give him "Good morning"? But Jackson's next remark somewhat changed the situation. Showing no irritation at being so coolly snubbed, he added, "I was just passing Mr. Everett's place this morning when he said, 'Jackson, if you see Mr. Topping on your way home, will you please give him this message?' " Mr. Jackson stated that he had replied that it would give him pleasure to be of service. " 'Ask Mr. Topping the next time he is passing my place to please bring his sledge hammer with him.' " Mr. Topping was visibly embarrassed. He said, "Go on over to the Lion, Jackson, and order a quart of beer. Have it set up to me. I am greatly obliged." Jackson proceeded toward the Lion somewhat impressed by the blacksmith's liberality. A whole quart of beer for such a trifling service was indeed generous.

Mr. Topping, glad of an excuse to call on his friend, at once removed his leather apron, put the sledge hammer over his shoulder and telling his helper, a man named Grimmer who was lower class and knew it and was also proud of the fact, that he would be back in an hour, he presently ar-

"Stopping at the blacksmith shop one morning before he had had time to get drunk."

rived at the Everett farm about one mile from his shop. Mr. Everett was pleased to see him. "Where are you going with the sledge?" he asked. Mr. Topping related the Jackson message. Mr. Everett said he had not seen the sailor and further expressed the opinion that no one else had ever seen him as much as a mile from the Red Lion while he had any money left. After discussing the matter in an attempt to find some reason for the sailor's conduct, one of them suddenly remembered that the date was April first, on which day most anything might happen. Mr. Topping returned, calling at the Lion with the intention of hitting Jackson with the sledge, but that worthy had finished the quart of beer and left. The landlord who was an apostle of the creed that, "Short credits make long friends," reminded Mr. Topping that he owed for one quart of beer.

Lower middle class women are not usually quite as stable as their more humble sisters; they at times develop temperament, have whims and notions which would not be tolerated by lower class husbands. Mrs. Topping or Helen had the notion that the teahouse had not been properly placed on the miniature lawn. They wanted it moved to an opposite corner. To this the husband and father was agreeable, but the teahouse, though small indeed, was still too heavy for him and journeyman blacksmith Grimmer to lift. As neither of them had ever

(29)

studied physics, they knew of no way to move any object which could not be raised by hand. But Mr. Topping had other knowledge which made him independent of science. In our village, coin of the realm, mostly in the form of large pennies, which feel like a lot of money even though they are not very potent in purchasing anything much worth having, together with a limited circulation of small silver coins, were the usual medium of exchange. There was, however, one other important medium which was often used in making payment. This was beer. If a farmer wanted his men to work overtime, he did not pay them time and a half, nor even the ordinary scale, but gave them beer. All of the farmers and some of the workmen's wives made beer. My mother made excellent beer. I know it was excellent because my father said it was. Personally, I have never liked beer.

In this emergency Mr. Topping crossed over to the Lion and ordered a gallon of beer to be served when enough men congregated to move the summerhouse and place it on another corner of the lawn. Soon several men had assembled and came over to see what service was needed. A very old man—Mr. Gosling, the husband of the village midwife—brought up the rear. Mr. Gosling did not know exactly what it was all about but he had heard beer mentioned and he knew a lot, if not all there was to be known, about beer. Mr. Topping directed the men to pick up the little building and place it in the new location which had been selected. With the exception of Mr. Gosling, the men stooped down and placed their fingers under the sill of the building. Mr. Gosling, a bit confused, stepped inside the house just as it was raised from the ground. When it was again at rest, he emerged and followed the others back to the Lion to drink his share of the beer.

―――――――――――――――――――――――――――――

Shortly before I reached my fifth birthday the Act of Parliament making education compulsory was passed. My school days terminated shortly before I was twelve years old, but I never knew when they began, for even while I lived the carefree life which enabled me to spend so much time watching the Topping family I was attending what was termed a school for part of the forenoon, and had been doing so since before I reached the age when one's comings and goings are a matter of mental registration. This so-called school, which was merely a playhouse, was conducted by a Mrs. Pinkham. Mrs. Pinkham was an industrious woman who lived in the last house at the south end of the village. There was a Mr. Pinkham, but ill-health, or possibly a natural disinclination for work, kept him inactive. There was a son, Tom Pinkham, who worked as a laborer on a farm; also a daughter, Jemima Pinkham, a girl of eleven or twelve years of age. Some eight or ten children attended Mrs. Pinkham's school, sent there more to be out of the way, no doubt, than for any educational advantages. Jemima was really our caretaker and teacher. She taught us some rhymes, the alphabet, how to tell the time and probably some other things which have never been entered to her credit. I still know the alphabet and can tell time by the clock, but the only one of Jemima's rhymes which I now recall is the one she should not have taught us, or the one I should most promptly have forgotten. However, I have not that kind of a mentality. I can remember a vast amount that I should never have learned but have forgotten nearly everything worth knowing that was ever drilled into me. Possibly my reader can benefit from the following:

Joe Muggins, he stood at his garden gate,
Minding his old grey moke,
When up came little Isabel
And thus to her husband she spoke:

"Where are you going, Joe Muggins?" she said,
"Where are you going?" said she.
Joe Muggins replied, "I'm going to town,
To sell this old donkey."

"When will you be back, Joe Muggins?" she said,
"When will you be back?" said she.
"Oh, I'll not be gone more'n an hour and a half
So cook me a bloater for tea."

He hadn't been gone an hour and a half,
To Smithfield to sell his donkey,
When thoughts of the bloater came into his head,
"I hope it's a soft roe," said he.

Joe Muggins, he died as it might be today,
His wife, she died next week,
Out of his grave there grew a large carrot
And out of hers, a leek.

They grew till they'd reached the top of the
*   grave;*
They grew till they'd grow no more;
They were then cut down and made into soup.
Which was given away to the poor.

The school was the Pinkham living room. While I do not recall, if I ever knew, the scale of compensation to Mrs. Pinkham, it was probably a penny a week or something very moderate; otherwise I would not have had the distinction of being one of her pupils.

As a further aid to the family support, Mrs. Pinkham held the office of rural carrier or postman for the village. As many of her clientele could not read, Mrs. Pinkham had the double responsibility of delivering and reading the correspondence. It is not probable that her contract with the Post Office Department required that she perform the latter service, but was the woman ever born with so little curiosity that she would not be willing to read her neighbor's correspondence when doing so was conferring a favor? The letters were left at Toppings, where a wooden mailbox for receiving letters was also located. I never learned why Topping figured in this governmental function. If Mrs. Pinkham could qualify to deliver the mail, why was it not left at her house in place of being carried on to Toppings? Possibly some unfathomable political influence was the reason for this division of responsibility. To facilitate the work of distribution, Mrs. Pinkham kept a donkey. About the time her—or Jemima's—pupils assembled, she would prepare to start out on her delivery service. She first went up to Toppings to pick up the mail with which she returned to the house. First she read the postcards, if there were any in the collection, and then she sorted the letters into an intelligent plan of her route. If none of the letters were for outlying points in the village, she would hitch up the donkey and go forth. If there was much mileage involved, she left the donkey at home, service without the donkey being much more rapid than when it was used. When the roads were wet and muddy and Mrs. Pinkham was making deliveries on foot, she wore what were called "pattens," a sort of skeleton ironwork which

"She would hitch up the donkey and go forth."

raised her soles some two inches from the ground.

Mrs. Pinkham had the only livery service in the village. Her donkey could be hired at any time regardless of her own needs or convenience at a shilling a day. While she had a complete monopoly, she did not weigh each separate opportunity to determine just "what the traffic would bear." However, her livery service was not in very great demand. East Anglians were not exactly "speed fiends"; nor were they much interested in transportation which was slower than walking. I recall that one day in winter with two or three inches of snow on the ground, Emma Tompkins, one of our young women of the village—being lower class the term "young lady" could never have been applied to Emma—had to go to town four miles distant for a bottle of medicine for some ailing member of her family. She engaged the donkey for the trip, started at daylight, and just as darkness was falling she arrived home, having made the eight miles in one day. Mrs. Pinkham knew her donkey; she rented it by the day and allowed those who hired it to develop the speed.

Up to the age of five, I attended Mrs. Pinkham's school but when I passed that momentous milestone I was taken from her establishment and sent to the public or Board School. This was indeed an important event. My brother Jimmy, who was my immediate senior, on this occasion acted as my caretaker and guardian. Jimmy was a loyal and devoted brother. Though but two years older than I, he fully sensed his responsibility. The school was about one mile from our house and served two villages. It mustered an attendance of slightly more than one hundred children. At the time I was enrolled, the school was in charge of a lady principal or mistress, as she was called, with an assistant mistress and two village girls who were called "pupil teachers." The mistress and her assistant were kindly indulgent young women; school was not so bad. Occasionally a child was punished, but never severely. I recall more clearly my first morning in school than I do the happenings of last week. A bell summoned us to our seats. School commenced at nine; the mistress rang a small bell for attention. School opened with prayer after which all the children joined in singing the hymn of which the following is the first verse:

> *Awake my soul and with the sun*
> *Thy daily stage of duty run.*
> *Shake off dull sloth, and joyful rise*
> *To pay thy morning sacrifice.*

The first and longest lesson of the day was Scripture or Bible study.

I was placed in the gallery class. We were seated on benches without any back supports. There were no desks, paper, nor even a slate for our class members. Our lessons were given on a blackboard by one of the "pupil teachers." The teacher also used a large framework with wires across it on which were strung large beads of different colors. We were taught to add and subtract by our teacher's sliding the beads on the wires. Division and multiplication would be taught in the next class. We were taught more rhymes but better selections than Jemima's "Joe Muggins"; also verses from the Psalms and whole chapters of the Proverbs of Solomon, Son of David, King of Israel. Solomon particularly enjoined us to get wisdom and understanding, and I am sure we did our best to follow his sound advice.

A few minutes before twelve the mistress would ring her small bell for attention and we would all rise and sing grace before dinner, as the noon meal was called. I think the grace and also the morning and evening hymns were changed with different principals, but the ones in use when I entered school were:

Before dinner:

Be present at our table, Lord,
Be here and everywhere adored,
These creatures bless and grant that we
May feast in Paradise with Thee.

After dinner, for which one hour was allowed, we were again called to attention and sang:

We thank Thee Lord for this our food
But praise Thee more for Jesus' blood,
Let manna to our souls be given,
The bread of life sent down from Heaven.

(37)

The school was under the direct management of a Board composed of men prominent in the two villages. These men acted, as did the magistrates, without direct compensation but did so gladly, no doubt, as it gave them opportunity to minimize the taxes or rates, as they were termed. The school, however, was still under close governmental supervision. It was soon learned that under the kindly woman mistress the morale of the school was not all that it might have been in the opinion of the supervisors. A change was made, and a master appointed to take charge, a decision which probably was reflected in the Board members' tax assessments in order to meet the higher salary of the master. The two good women were no doubt demoted for lack of efficiency.

A Mr. Danforth appeared as the new schoolmaster, with his wife as his assistant. Mr. Danforth had apparently been advised that he was being run up against a very hard situation. He came supplied with a whole bundle of heavy canes with which he planned to raise the efficiency level of his young charges. He started his course of discipline at once and with wonderful impartiality went right down the line. The youngest children were five, and but few of the older ones were more than twelve years of age. They were neither old enough nor sufficiently well organized to put up any resistance. The girls fared no better than the boys. They were the potential mothers of another generation and they needed proper training and discipline. The form of punishment was to call the child, or children, as Mr. Danforth seldom bothered to pick up his cane for one child and often had a queue waiting, some having been sent out by the pupil teachers who became very alert to what was expected of them, or by Mrs. Danforth, the assistant. The child was told to extend its hand which was promptly struck with the cane; then the other hand was extended. Sometimes as many as six or eight cuts were given, leaving that many welts on the hands of the poor child. The incorrigibles were thoroughly thrashed all over the body to boot. As Mr. Danforth moved around through the classes, he would tap slow-witted ones on the head or knuckles with a rule which he carried with him. As none of the contemporaries of my youth, to my knowledge, ever achieved any considerable measure of fame or notoriety, we may conclude that Mr. Danforth's bundle of canes did not affect their mental development to good or bad end.

While brother Jimmy was my caretaker, brother Billy also attended school. He had been drawn back to school by the passage of the act after working for two or three years. He was then nearly twelve years of age. One of the babies which had died had been born between his birth and that of brother Jimmy. One day Mrs. Danforth, with the loyalty of a good wife and perhaps a desire to help her busy husband, undertook to administer a little corporal punishment herself. Her victim, or nemesis, was brother Billy. He was called out in front of his class. The first cut was given; resentment was instantaneous. A well-directed twist of Billy's foot around Mrs. Danforth's ankles took that lady's feet from under her. She crumpled, making a most undignified collapse, striking her head heavily on the floor. Mrs. Danforth was indisputably lower middle class, but simplicity of dress still prevailed on that social ledge. Mrs. Danforth was not in somersaulting costume. She lost consciousness from the blow on the head, or she fainted. Anyway, she became a jumbled mass. Mr. Danforth was not equal to the job of picking her up and carrying her out. The pupil teachers, girls in their teens, were rendered dumb and almost prostrated by the occurrence. The larger boys, while they could have separately carried an arm or a leg, had not had training in first-aid or relief work. Mrs. Danforth was revived on the schoolroom floor and finally with her husband's assistance was removed to their cottage, which adjoined the schoolhouse. Mr. Danforth then returned and took up the charge. Poor brother Billy was beaten to a near pulp and sent home. The matter of his insubordination and assault was taken before the School Board. That body decided that brother Billy's conduct had been unspeakable and un-English; that he was potentially a murderer and in spite of the Act of Parliament requiring his presence in school or his parents' presence in jail as an alternative until he was thirteen years of age or had passed the fourth standard, he was expelled. He returned to the job from which he had been taken.

Brother Jimmy and I got along very well with Mr. Danforth, not because he liked us, but for the reason that he evidently regarded us as bad material. He was being subjected to some underhanded persecution in the form of stones through his windows at night. He had been stoned one Sunday night when returning from church with his wife and on one occasion when the snow was in good workable form, both he and his wife had been nearly annihilated. Their umbrellas which they raised for protection were smashed; Mr. Danforth lost his hat and no doubt felt that he nearly lost his life. Our family, who had nothing whatever to do with the attacks, were probably blamed for most of this misfortune. Doubtless Mr. Danforth concluded that not much would be gained in bringing more fuel to the flame by thrashing Jimmy and me. But his general policy remained unchanged. He got results, however, and results either secured promotion for him or he decided that our village did not contain the possibilities he had hoped for and asked for a transfer. After Mr. Danforth left, the school went back—or forward according to the viewpoint—and woman teachers were again installed.

My clothing at this time consisted almost entirely of articles my older brothers had outgrown. Many of these had been handed right down the line through my three older brothers and finally to me. Some of them had become veritable heirlooms; knickerbockers which had seen years of service, usually made of corduroy and almost indestructible. Wearing a pair of much patched knickers, something in the place of a vest—possibly it would be an old scarf wound around me and pinned in the back to serve as the vest of the occasion—then a blouse, with us called a "slop," made of a local fabric called "drabette," and under all, a cotton shirt which my mother had made, bare-legged, I would start out for school with the parting injunction to run until I got warm. The luxury of woollen underwear or of any underwear was unknown to us. I do not recall ever being seriously inconvenienced by the cold, but on account of going barehanded and sometimes playing in the snow, my hands would be badly chapped all winter. I was also bothered at times with chilblains on my feet. My father's remedies for the curse of chilblains were beating the affected part with prickly holly or holding the feet close enough to the fire to scorch them, either of which remedies I soon concluded were worse than the chilblains. One day when my father's work took him to town, he reported to my mother on his return that he had seen some fine-looking shirts for sale at elevenpence each. Mother was much relieved that he had not fallen for the "bargain," for she could buy the material for a shirt for half that price, and Mother had not learned to place a cash value on her time.

Since I have grown up, I have learned a little and heard a great deal about dietetics and the importance of a properly balanced diet. My mother exploded all these theories before they were written. She never heard of dietetics, vitamins, or calories. A lecturer on such a subject would not have received an audience from her. She would have defined a balanced diet as the amount of food needed to balance the hunger that was felt at the time. What about the Children of Israel? Did not they live on manna alone for forty years? When our fare was unusually plain, I have heard my father say, "Today we'll put on a streak of lean," adding that no child could be properly developed if his flesh was composed entirely of fat. If spinach had been invented prior to my childhood, it had not found its way into our garden. I doubt that it would have made any appeal to my mother, whose ideas of food values were biased strongly in favor of those containing real substance. And yet, in his professional capacity, I never saw a doctor, and none ever saw me until I was grown up. Members of that honorable profession could, insofar as my need of their services during my childhood and youth were concerned, have found time for a lot of postgraduate courses. Our food was more than ninety per cent bread. For breakfast we had bread and milk, the milk skimmed to a degree that made the invention of cream separators quite unnecessary. Or possibly we had "sugar sop," which was prepared as for bread and milk, each child breaking a bowlful of bread. Hot water was then poured over it and a modicum of sugar added. Or sometimes we had "skilly," which was prepared the same as the other dishes with a small amount of fat added, also pepper and salt before the hot water was poured over it. I did not care much for the "sugar sop"; it appeared to be such a baby food. However, we always ate what was prepared for us. As we were never consulted, we knew nothing about expressing a preference. Our bowls were of different sizes and all of different colors, which circumstance in no way detracted from the flavor of their contents.

For dinner—the noon meal—we had dumplings, not the kind that are associated with fricasseed chicken (these are drop dumplings) but real substantial dumplings made and formed into shape before going into the boiler. They were from four to six inches in diameter and were as good as bread when cold. Slices of toasted dumplings were a favorite dish with us children for breakfast. We usually had potatoes, which we ate with bread, a most glaring dietetic irregularity of which we were of course wholly ignorant. Often we had turnips, usually the yellow or Swedish variety. If anyone ever discovered anything that equals a dinner of grilled herring, yellow turnips and potatoes mashed together, I have not been fortunate enough to hear about it. During the summer months we had cabbage and scarlet runner kidney beans. These beans are usually described on hotel bills as "French beans," the English being willing to give the French the credit for producing anything not overly desirable. Visitors to England any time between June and Christmas will find it hard to dodge these beans served under one of their numerous aliases. Sometimes we had stewed rabbit, occasionally pig's fry, as certain internal organs of the pig were called, sometimes part of a herring for each child, and quite infrequently a small piece of meat. A great treat was the small pieces of fat pork called scraps from which the lard had been rendered. Eaten with mustard, these "scraps" were a real delicacy. For Christmas we had roast beef and plum pudding. But we never received enough meat or fish to in any manner affect our development. Bread, the "staff of life," was our dependence. During the winter we sometimes had pea soup. Mother would procure a half of a pig's head, which would be cooked in a large boiler with dried peas. Half an hour before dinner was to be served some dumplings would be dropped in; then for two or three days it would be reheated, and each time more dumplings would be added. This was luxurious living and more than could be afforded except at infrequent intervals. We would gorge with soup and dumplings till we were red in the face and breathless.

Supper was always a cold meal. Bread and butter with a ratio of about half an ounce of butter to a lineal foot of bread. Small helpings of Dutch cheese made from skim milk and wholly devoid of fat but no doubt containing other valuable and nutritive elements. It would be hard to imagine such a fine people as the Dutch exporting any food commodity which they would not have been willing to serve at home. We often had raw onions; these were supposed to be very good for us. I have never found anything else quite as good as a help to the mastication of dry bread. In the summer time we also had green onions, radishes, and cress.

From the age of four—and no doubt four years previous to that time—until I was ten, I lived the life of a prince. Not many, I am sure, can look back on a happier childhood. Up to the age of ten, happiness, or the lack of it, is certainly the only condition a child can understand. I have no argument with those who advocate a properly balanced diet for children. In my case it was not needed. On the simple fare of my childhood, I developed a physique which carried me through years of hardship and exposure much greater than falls to the lot of the average man, and to those so fortunate as to be born in

America, quite seldom. At my present age I find it expedient to be careful of my food selections but even more careful of the quantity. My mother and father lived to be seventy-nine and eighty-four respectively, and I have no reason to assume that had they had a great deal of knowledge of dietetics, they would have lived much longer. Their average age was probably as great as the average of those who have been most proficient in the science of food in relation to health and longevity. While the family health always hovered around the one hundred per cent mark, my mother was an ardent advocate of the use of "spring medicine." She had a formula for mixing brimstone and treacle, as sulphur and molasses were termed. This is an abominable concoction. Mother served it in tablespoon doses. I would run and yell at the sight of the jar which contained it but always ended by swallowing my dose. Epsom salts were kept on hand for "bellyache" emergencies and sweet oil for burns, but beyond that Mother was disposed to trust in Providence or consult Mrs. Gosling.

Our house fronted on the main London highway, or turnpike. There was no front yard; the door opened immediately on the road. For protection at night—the entire household furniture and equipment were probably worth less than ten pounds—the one window on the ground floor front was supplied with thick wooden shutters which overlapped and were secured by a heavy bolt which went through the window frame. The front door was secured by a lock with a massive key, which key my mother would drop down brother Jimmy's back inside his shirt when he had nosebleed, a trouble to which he was for a time addicted. When Mrs. Gosling heard of the matter, however, she prescribed for the nosebleeding by advising my mother to procure a piece of red silk thread and have nine knots tied in it by nine different virgins and place it around Jimmy's neck. This charm proved immediately effective, and no more nosebleeding occurred.

As our house was in the center of the village and only removed from the crossroad by the width of the Topping premises, we were surrounded by the village life. During play hours the road in front of our house was filled with the neighborhood children.

Usually in the evenings a small group of men would assemble on the crossing, each intending to enter the Lion and purchase a mug of beer when everybody was present and the maximum of social intercourse could be secured with the beer for a penny or three halfpence, according to whether the guests could afford XXX or could indulge only in XX beer. Vehicles were constantly stopping at the Lion. Carriers' carts laden with farm produce and an occasional passenger or two, loads of grain or hay en route to market, herds of cattle—which I would view from the inside of our house—and droves of sheep passed by. The pigs were usually hauled in carts. Pigs on account of their tendency to run in circles, an effect caused by their wish to keep an eye on the herder, were hard to drive. An occasional tramp passed by, wearing shoes with very thick soles. Tramping was a profession, and those who followed it were properly equipped for the needs of their trade. Begging, however, when practiced on the average lower class members, was not a very remunerative calling. The rewards of charity dispensers must necessarily be the thrills they receive from making their dispensations, and most of our villagers preferred the thrill of a need supplied.

Next to the Snobeys, in a southerly direction, lived two elderly couples who had no children at home. Their children were probably grown and settled on their own account; actual childless women were rare. Beyond, there was a small one-story cottage where lived the widow Sprunt. Mrs. Sprunt had four children, two of whom, Isabella and Ellis, were about my age. As I never knew which of the two was the elder, it is probably safe to conclude that they were twins. They both attended Mrs. Pinkham's school at the time I was enrolled as a member of that institution. Mrs. Sprunt took in washing, although whose washing it could be, it would be hard to say as everybody in the village did their own washing with the exception of the few who kept servants to wash their clothes for them.

Next to the home of the Sprunt family was the village shop conducted by the sisters Susan and Martha Lark. Susan and Martha did very well with their little shop until Susan fell in love with Mr. Smith who lived next door south. Mr. Smith was a natural son of Mrs. Bundy, the wife of the Class B carpenter. There was some romance and a good deal of mystery surrounding Mr. Smith. It was not very unusual for a child's history to be somewhat shrouded in mystery, but in most cases the romance was gone before the baby arrived and the further mystery of who would provide for the new one was added to the case. In the case of Mr. Smith, however, romance, interest or some rather dull sense of duty had prompted someone in the background to provide this illegitimate son of Mrs. Bundy with a very good education. Mr. Smith manifested his good breeding and education in his every word and act. None ever attempted familiarity with Mr. Smith. He was never addressed by his first name, whatever that may have been, and he did not frequent the Lion. He was a gentleman, and an English "gentleman" is a really fine product. He is not confined to any class; in fact he would be insensible to class distinctions, but the "climbers," of which there are all too many, are at all times trying to ride on his shoulders into the light which he has created. They wish to be regarded as "gentlemen" even though they themselves know that they lack the qualifications and instincts of a gentleman. If Mr. Smith's status as a gentleman was an hereditary one, it would be necessary to go back further than his immediate father to establish that fact, as the mere instance of his illegitimacy would deprive his father of that qualification. Mr. Smith was unquestionably very conscious of the "detour" in the line of his descent but he bore the indignity unflinchingly. He could not—his instincts would have rebelled against such a course—associate with the uneducated villagers; those higher in the social scale would most certainly not recognize him. It was Mr. Smith's duty and privilege to establish himself in the social life of the community and by his life and conduct attempt to live down the misfortune of his birth. One day when I was returning heavy laden from an errand on which my mother had sent me, I was overtaken by Mr. Smith who took the (to me) heavy basket from my arm and carried it nearly to our door but then handed it back to avoid the risk of receiving any thanks other than those I was able to express. Mrs. Bundy, his mother, was a very attractive woman. Even at age five I realized that and I have never been considered precocious. After she married Bundy—and there may have been "inducements" to bring about that event, though certainly none should have been needed to get any man to marry such a good-looking woman who had one child already as evidence of her complete normality —she gave birth to another son. But when she saw how poorly her second son compared with her first, she concluded that she had been married at the wrong time or had married the wrong man, and ceased to be a potentiality insofar as Mrs. Gosling's services as a midwife were concerned.

Except for the minister and possibly one other, Mr. Smith was the best-educated man in the village. Lacking any competition for the various positions, he held every office in the village which required much scholastic knowledge for its fulfillment. He was truant officer after that office was created, he was health officer, secretary of the lodge. He was tall and athletic and could lay his hand on the top of a gate and vault over it; he would walk several miles just for exercise. His contemporaries never walked for exercise; if they did any walking, it was a part of their day's work for which they were paid. Most of them, however, would have walked further for a pint of beer than Mr. Smith walked for exercise. One day when Mr. Smith came home for his midday meal, his mother met him with the startling information that the shirt which he had worn the previous week and which she had just washed and "hung out" had been taken from the line. Mr. Smith had a trained mind; he knew what to do in an emergency. He first inquired of the neighbors if any strangers had been seen in the vicinity and was told that a tramp had passed going south about an hour earlier. To chase a tramp who had but an hour's start was, to Mr. Smith, hardly a sporting proposition, but he started out. He soon overhauled a tramp, but the tramp displayed no evidence of an extra shirt or even of any shirt. Mr. Smith decided to search the tramp and to start at his skin and work outward. The first thing he found going in that direction was the wet shirt, which he recovered, leaving the tramp taking a sun bath fifty years before the beneficial effect of such treatment was known to the tramp or anyone else.

Mr. Smith was attracted to Miss Susan Lark. Being a reasoning man, he may have sensed a position of greater security as the husband of the least attractive of the two very plain spinsters who kept the shop. Also, this was about as good a compromise as he could hope to ever make with the social situation of which he was a victim. His different positions were semipolitical, and not many other openings existed for a man of his type in our village. In due time they were married, and the name of the firm was changed to that of Smith and Lark. At once it became evident that what the business had lacked was the male influence. A new policy was adopted. More shelves were installed; the parlor was sacrificed to make additional room for more stock. Piece goods and even ready-made shoes were added to the line of merchandise. Credit was offered to those who needed it, and while the villagers did not know much about credit, they promptly realized that they all needed it. A fire would not have moved goods more rapidly than they disappeared under this previously unheard-of stimulus. No merchant had ever before tried such a daring experiment on our people. They responded with most gratifying enthusiasm. The clientele was extended to the adjoining villages. Extending credit to people who have never before known such a luxury or temptation was all at the risk of the seller. Most of the customers did not earn more than twelve or thirteen shillings a week, if they worked all the time, and they could not always work when it rained. They operated without family budgets, and but few of them could have correctly defined the word "reserves." Soon it dawned on Mr. Smith that his new policy had not been well considered. The villagers in the capacity of debtors

manifested actual stubbornness. Soon the firm of
Smith and Lark were in financial difficulties. But
just at that time, Mr. Smith, who had retained all of
his secretarial positions in spite of the heavy demands on his time and strength in the field of merchandising, when out investigating a case of typhoid
got so close to his work that he himself contracted
the fever and died, leaving his widow and her sister
Martha to extricate themselves as best they could
from a very embarrassing situation.

Between the Bundy cottage and Mrs. Pinkham's
home and school were some four or five other cottages, the occupants of which, other than the Gos-
lings, did not enter my life. While Mr. Gosling had
but little concern in the village life, other than to
be on hand when beer was being poured, his wife was
in many respects the most important person in the
village as she was the official midwife in a community which, if they believed in birth control, had but
a most limited knowledge of its practice. Most of
the married women did their full duty to God and
their country, while "accidents" among the un-
married women were frequent. Had Mrs. Gosling
possessed any knowledge that would have been helpful in preventing them—which it is safe to conclude
she did not—her professional interest and pride
would have restrained her from making it known.
Besides officiating at all births, Mrs. Gosling was on
hand to do the "laying out" at all deaths. She was

often consulted in cases of sickness and would appear carrying a large bottle of turpentine. She exuded an odor of turpentine. The patient, whose status when Mrs. Gosling took charge was immediately changed to that of victim, was given a large dose of Epsom salts, followed by a few drops of turpentine in sugar. The turpentine was supposed to stir the victim's kidneys into any action they were still capable of performing. He was then subjected to a sweat by any process that would produce one. Mrs. Gosling was strong for elimination although she had never heard the word. Under her ministrations the patient would soon be better or dead, and usually they were better. For pains and rheumatics Mrs. Gosling prescribed hot red flannel. White flannel was, in her opinion, wholly lacking in curative virtue. In extreme cases a mustard plaster was applied. She was the only person in the village who could apply a mustard plaster without removing the patient's skin. But all of Mrs. Gosling's knowledge—which was not written in Latin—was closely guarded. She was gifted with extraordinary powers of discernment in the matter of family resemblance. She could tell the father of a baby an hour after it was born with unfailing accuracy. "I dew declare," she would exclaim, "it's the very image of the young master—" a statement which would cost the young master or his parents at least five pounds. The young mother, then being so well endowed, someone would marry her for her money. The bridegroom had probably never seen five pounds at one time before in his life. No particular resentment was felt, and nearly anyone would agree that a little good blood would not lower the general average of any family.

While Mrs. Gosling's knowledge of dietetics was no greater than that of my mother's, she did know precisely what was needed for new mothers. A generous service of onion broth was the first food the patient received and, as they usually survived and in most cases repeated the offense, it is quite reasonable to assume that there is merit in the treatment. After that they were put on a diet of gruel—I am sure there is no merit in gruel—a cereal product made from oats with only the husks removed. Served without sugar or milk, it is absolutely objectionable. Gruel was usually fed to anyone who for any reason was indisposed. No faith cure was ever as effective. In the case of new mothers but a very few meals of gruel would be necessary to convince them that they were again ready to resume life's burdens, and they would be up and eating a smoked herring or some bread and cheese, self-preservation being the dominant motive.

Mrs. Gosling, besides being the village nurse, mortician, and "doctor of sorts," was also its chief genealogical authority. She was familiar with the history of every family in the village and had a knowledge of everything of importance which had

(57)

happened there since the time her grandmother was a child, which time extended back to the early part of the previous century. Most anyone would be placed at a disadvantage if they challenged a gossip who knew the foibles of their great-grandmother's half cousins. While at that time a man might marry his first cousin, marriage with a sister of his deceased wife was, for some deep biological reason, prohibited.

Our village, for religious as well as educational purposes, was combined with one adjoining. Separately the villages afforded only tolerable "livings" for a minister. Combined, they yielded an income of some six hundred pounds annually. This was a magnificent salary. The minister was one of the only two in the combined villages who could have been regarded as upper middle class. The family kept four servants, had a coachman who wore a silk hat. They lived in a fine home with a broad expanse of lawn in front of its French windows. The minister's wife had two bracelets, one of gold, the other of silver. These were worn in accordance with the importance of the "occasion" and when there was no "occasion" were not worn at all. The religious needs of the separate communities were served by holding morning service in one parish and evening service in the other, alternating each Sunday. The services were entirely ritualistic. If the minister ever offered an extemporaneous prayer, it was probably one of thankfulness that he had been born to such high

"Mr. Snobey was clerk of the village church."

estate. He was blessed with a large family of children, so large indeed that he had had the family carriage constructed on the lines of a carryall, or bus, with a seat across the front and on each side to make seating space for the coachman, the minister, his wife—with or without the bracelets—the nurse, and the numerous children. The children were dressed in marvelous clothing. The little boys wore white collars turned back to their shoulder blades. The little girls looked like bundles of ruffles. But they never watched Mr. Topping make a horseshoe from a short length of iron bar; most likely they never had pea soup and dumplings; they knew nothing of what went on at the Lion, their nurse most probably directing their gaze in the opposite direction when the carriage drove by that famous hostelry. White collars and ruffles will not compensate a child for the loss of the common natural joys of life.

Mr. Snobey was the clerk of the village church. He was able to read, an advantage many of his contemporaries did not enjoy. The minister would race through the service with almost incredible speed, but his manner, insofar as Mr. Snobey was concerned, was not infectious. It took Mr. Snobey nearly as long to say amen as it did the minister to recite the prayer. Banns were published for three consecutive Sundays before a marriage—a formality which sometimes allowed the stork to "beat the game." Christenings were held occasionally, the minister preferring to bunch the christenings, for to perform that ceremony he had to walk to the opposite end of the church where the baptismal font was located. Mothers were "churched," or given a special prayer, when they returned to church after a birth.

While a Dissenter might avoid the church during his life, he could not escape it at death for the reason that there was no place to be buried except in the churchyard where none but the properly ordained clergy were allowed to officiate. When a death occurred in the village, Mr. Snobey, as clerk of the church, was notified. He would leave his work— that of a farm laborer—and proceed to the church. If the deceased was an adult, Mr. Snobey would toll the largest bell in the belfry, a stroke every minute, standing with his watch in his hand. If the deceased was a child, he would toll the smallest bell. Just when a child became an adult was a matter for Mr. Snobey's discretion. He also dug the graves and, as far as I ever knew, he selected the sites. At the time set for the funeral the minister would appear at the churchyard, driven by his coachman wearing the silk hat, and conduct the service. There was but one service for adults, regardless of class, religious creeds, or church affiliations. Nothing was left to the judgment or initiative of the minister. The service was read from the Book of Common Prayer. It had been prepared to suit all occasions, possibly approved by

Queen Elizabeth herself or her venerated father, Henry the Eighth. The coffin was carried on the shoulders of friends of the deceased. The service was brief and rendered more so by the minister's familiarity with the ritual which enabled him to gallop through the short prayers. After the funeral it was customary to return to the former home of the deceased and partake of tea and cake.

Watching Mr. Snobey dig a grave was at all times a matter of interest. The small churchyard had been used as a burial ground for centuries. Wherever Mr. Snobey dug, before he was down the regulation six feet, he would usually encounter bones. These bones we would use as playthings or we would speculate as to the part of the body where they had belonged and the age and sex of their former possessor.

Weddings were held in the church and were conducted by the minister, who did not expect to receive any added compensation for this service and on that score was never taken by surprise. After the wedding all of the several bells in the belfry were rung in celebration. The length of time they were rung depended mainly upon how much beer the groom or his friends were willing to provide. On these occasions Mr. Snobey had assistance, the beer in prospect being the inducement. If enough beer were forthcoming, the bells would be rung all night.

The village record of births, marriages, and deaths was kept in the vestry of the church. The ministry of the church was in the nature of a profession. Wealthy fathers, holding entailed or copyhold estates which must of necessity be handed down to the eldest son, would provide for other sons by having them educated for a profession, secure them commissions in the Army or the Indian Service, or where proper political influence could be exerted, get them a "living," the term applied to an appointment to a church. Apparently the matter of their spiritual fitness was not always the first requisite. Some noblemen controlled a number of "livings" which could be distributed to those selected somewhat as post office and port collector jobs are distributed in America by successful politicians to their faithful supporters, with the exception, however, that a "living" was a gift for the life of the fortunate recipient. It will be seen that a gift of six hundred pounds a year for life was a plum well worthy of acceptance, in particular when it also included the occupancy of an attractive vicarage and the discounts and emoluments to which ministers were entitled. In order to have properly administered to the spiritual needs of his parishioners, our minister should have employed a curate or assistant pastor. A competent one could no doubt have been secured for a pound a week, but the minister needed all of his generous stipend to care for and properly educate his large family, and perhaps the lady possessing two bracelets was hoping someday to own a third one.

With salvation free, however, there were those who refrained from accepting it through the medium of the Established Church. In our village there was a Primitive Methodist chapel. The term "church" could be applied only to the Church of England. This chapel had an attendance far in excess of that of the church, and later I was to enjoy its many advantages.

During the harvest season my mother and all of the children not profitably employed went gleaning somewhat as did Ruth in the Bible story, but Mother was better equipped than was Ruth for such a venture as she had a large family of small children whose eyes were good and not far above earth level—a very helpful factor in locating stray ears. We would sally forth after a farmer had raked his fields both ways with the hope of not missing an ear, and find good picking. The horserake would not catch ears in a furrow or any depression of the ground. We took our dinner with us. My sisters, Earley and Tilley, and I would be loaded in the coach cart, a small but substantial sort of four-wheel baby wagon, and hauled to the field. The grain gleaned through the day would be cut close to the ear, put in a sack, and the sack loaded on the coach cart. While I started the day gloriously by being hauled in the cart, this was done only to permit more speed in getting to the gleaning fields. I finished the day as extra horse, helping brother Jimmy pull the cart or pushing behind. One of my sisters was carried in her mother's arms, the other on top or under the sack of wheat according to the safety demands of the occasion. This wheat, in particular after a rain, did not make exactly Grade A flour, but we had not been raised to be critical. After gleaning was finished, the man who owned the threshing machine in the village set a day for threshing the gleanings. Having reduced our wheat to the condition of grain in sacks, it was taken to Dabney's mill and ground into flour. This supply would carry us part way through the winter and in fact sometimes lasted until it became "mitey," its low quality no doubt tending to hasten that development.

When flour was bought, it was delivered in twenty-stone—280-pound—sacks and was emptied into a hutch from which my mother drew her requirements on Tuesdays and Fridays. The oven was not large enough to bake a week's supply of bread in one day. We were not fed new bread as we would eat too much of it. The bread supply was kept a little ahead of requirements to allow it to become properly aged. Even when we went gleaning or picking blackberries—of which my mother made jam—the household duties had to be carried on as usual. This was done in the evening when it was too dark to glean or to pick blackberries. Washing and ironing had to be done in the same way.

After father had come home for his late supper—

usually a red herring and bread—he never said, "Where is the salad?" or "What are we having for dessert?" Mother would by the light of the candle (paraffin lamps had not yet come into general use) repair our tattered garments for the next day's service. When an article of clothing was worn beyond possible repair, Mother would remove the "good patches" and cut out all usable portions for patching something else.

Another help toward the family's support was that of picking acorns to sell to the farmers for fattening pigs. Oak trees grew for the most part in the hedgerows, and the pigs could not very well be herded around to do their own picking. We picked them up after they had fallen to the ground, sometimes very cold work for the hands, but I was shown how to swing my arms and clap my hands against my shoulders to restore or promote circulation. We could pick acorns only on Saturdays as the summer holidays—one month during gleaning season—were over.

In spite of the strenuous life my mother lived, she was not the run-down haggard creature one might expect to see. She was an efficiency expert long before efficiency became a science and its proponents had their names on payrolls. Mother had sparkling eyes and rosy cheeks. She constantly regretted that the shortness of the day prevented her from doing all that she saw needed to be done. My father would spend the evening, if there was any daylight left after he had finished his supper, working in the miniature garden back of the house. We drew our water from a well at the rear of one of the neighbor's gardens. We did not keep a pig, but many of our neighbors did. A pig would have found pickings rather scant after we children had gone through a meal. These pigstys, as also the open toilets, were in threatening proximity to the well. We knew but little about sanitation, and if Mr. Smith noticed the arrangement, he said nothing, preferring to wait until there was real cause for his interference.

Most of the villagers believed in signs and had faith in "charms." The use of the red silk thread recommended by Mrs. Gosling for brother Jimmy's nosebleeding was a well-authenticated case of the efficacy of "charms." Belief in ghosts was also quite general; there was so much evidence available to support this belief that only the most foolish of persons would have challenged it. Most charms, however, needed a lot of what is now termed Christian Science to secure worth-while results.

As I have stated, diagonally across the road crossing from the blacksmith shop, was the Red Lion, a a public house, but the term "public house" does not adequately describe the Red Lion. It was an establishment, almost an institution. While it did not claim, as so many places and shops in England do, that it had been patronized by royalty, royalty could

"Diagonally across the road from the blacksmith shop was the
Red Lion."

have been very well served indeed had it stopped at the place, and neither royalty nor anyone else could have embarrassed its landlord. The license under which the Red Lion operated was owned by one of the brewing companies and was a very valuable concession. The landlord was a Mr. Crawshay, a capable man who had a very capable and buxom wife. Mr. Crawshay's first responsibility was to the brewing company which owned the license. Selling beer at wholesale was their business, and if any men in England understood their business it was the brewers. Had it been possible to instill the same amount of business acumen and enterprise into all lines of British trade as was almost invariably manifested by its brewers, all the rest of the world would long ago have been British Colonies. To this day they are among the master minds of the kingdom.

The Crawshays were staunch adherents of the Established Church, and why not? They were engaged in a business which was regarded as eminently respectable, that of selling beer to people who should have spent their money for food or other necessities which their families constantly lacked. The Crawshays had but two children; they could no doubt have well afforded to have had twenty children, and at that they would have been one short of the village record at that time. Their two children were girls, or rather young women, named Tottie and Elvina. Tottie, the elder of the daughters, was a youthful replica of her buxom mother. Elvina, the younger sister, was a "pupil teacher" at the Board School and received four shillings a week salary for that service. Elvina was very pretty but of an entirely different type than her sister. She had delicate and refined features and did not resemble either of her parents. Mrs. Gosling could no doubt have delivered a worthwhile dissertation on this striking family dissimilarity but Mrs. Gosling enjoyed a drink of beer almost as much as her husband did and never expressed opinions inimical to her own interests.

Although there appeared to exist a sort of community of interest between the church and the brewing companies, the minister was never seen at the Red Lion. The public houses or their landlords exerted a strong political influence, but the minister who had a job for life, contingent upon his continued good behavior, did not need to consider politics on his own account. Ministers, however, were almost invariably staunch Conservatives. The brewers were important factors in local affairs. They were usually leaders in civic and charitable movements; they had money to spend, and civic and charitable activities need plenty of money. They seldom ranked lower than upper middle class, frequently upper class, and to some extent they invaded the nobility. They all hoped, on account of the quality of their product, that they would at some time be at least knighted, and this honor was not infrequently bestowed on those who had not inherited titles. The beer dispensed at the Lion was said to be of uniformly good quality. My father claimed that the beer my mother made was far superior, but father was a biased critic, his bias being created partly by the fact that my mother's beer cost only about one third of what Mr. Crawshay charged for that which he dispensed at the Lion.

During the day Mr. Crawshay and Tottie took care of the trade with a little help at times from the mother. In the evening Elvina, home from her teaching, also attended bar. Mr. Crawshay was obliged to spend part of his time in the capacity of host visiting with his patrons. The Lion was the clearinghouse for all news—local, national, and foreign—although the vision of the callers or guests was for the most part quite limited on matters outside of their own country and even outside of their own county. But few had ever been to London, one hundred miles distant, and many had never been twenty miles from the place where they were born. No lack of knowledge, however, will prevent a man from having opinions and—after drinking a few mugs of beer—from expressing them. Mr. Crawshay manifested unusual tact in handling those who would have stopped drinking beer to carry on an argument. But keeping the stream of social intercourse flowing evenly with the flow of beer did not permit of Mr. Crawshay's leaving the barroom when it was well filled with thirsty patrons. Beer served in the general barroom—sometimes called the taproom—was brought in in very thick mugs. The mugs were of a pale yellow color with a wide brown rim at the top. Many of the "guests" chewed tobacco, and the brown rim of the mug was probably intended to conceal any lip marks which would otherwise have shown. The lip marks were there all right, but what the eye does not see the mind does not ponder on. Most of the patrons of the Lion wore full beards and mustaches. The beer was brought from the cellar with high tops of foam easily produced by holding the mug a distance below the tap. In later years machines were installed, and barmaids had only to pull a lever to start the flow. Beer, as I understand, and anyway as the patrons of the Lion understood, rapidly deteriorates when exposed to the air. Patrons did not wait for the foam to condense to liquid but plunged into the mugs as soon as the beer was served. Their mustaches would be immersed in the foam and to some extent in the liquid. The men were very skillful in twisting their tongues around one half of the mustache and sucking the beer and foam from it; then the same clever twist, something like a cow's tongue around a tuft of grass, and the other side would be relieved of its dripping. There was some opportunity, which Mr. Crawshay as a staunch church member could never have availed himself of, for giving slightly short measure as the customer could not see where the foam ended and the liquid commenced, and if they waited for the foam to liquefy their beer would be flat.

On Saturday nights in particular, when drinking was more free, the men would joke with Tottie and Elvina. Tottie could meet any and all comers and if any dared become too familiar could put them in their places with a few properly chosen remarks. But poor Elvina could not parry their coarse jokes but blushed and retreated in confusion. Elvina on one occasion was absent from the village for a short time, possibly visiting relatives, attending a bar-maid's convention, or spending a short time in a finishing school. The Monday following her return a strange garment appeared on the Crawshay clothesline. Monday was washday with everybody; there were no Jews or Seventh Day Adventists in our village. Sunday was Sunday, and Monday was the day following—no dispute between the Established Church and the Methodists on that score. This garment drew attention before it had time to dry. Criticism from the women was immediate and hostile; they did not want any such an idea introduced into the village. They foresaw more work on washdays and much less comfort on all days. The innocent grey calico garment was considered, in connection with the long skirts worn at the time, as being an inexcusable affectation. They quickly traced the notion back to Elvina and told that young woman that they wanted none of her advanced ideas. But Elvina stood her ground. Intuition, heredity, or some other invisible influence prompted Elvina's thoughts as to what constituted proper coverage for the form divine. Her stubbornness, however, created considerable resentment, and resentment in the minds of potential patrons has never helped anyone's business.

The women had pockets in all the long skirts which they wore and of which they usually wore three or four. These pockets were handy for storing extra diapers, handkerchiefs, teething rings for the baby, and any other small articles. The women could be seen in the Lark shop making purchases and payment. It was only during the short time that the firm was Smith and Lark that cash in hand was not necessary. They would lift the outer two or three skirts and extract their purse from the pocket of the innermost one. The purse would usually contain several of the large pennies, perhaps a shilling and a sixpence. These good women would have been real problems for a pickpocket.

As I have stated, with the exception of the Topping premises, we lived on a corner where a local road crossed the London highway. There were no cottages across the road from our house. This space was a meadow owned by a farmer named Rabbit, or Captain Rabbit as he was known. The Captain was

"Certainly any man who had successfully circumnavigated the globe
with the ships of that day and age was entitled to
a few opinions of his own."

an elderly man who, after many years at sea, had retired from that arduous calling and had taken up farming. What Captain Rabbit did not know about farming was a leading subject in the conversation at the Red Lion. He had many very original ideas, and the one thing he most emphatically declined to accept was advice. Certainly any man who had successfully circumnavigated the globe with the ships of that day and age was entitled to a few opinions of his own. Captain Rabbit was typical of the navigators of the day; he wore bushy grey whiskers—and lots of them; he talked in resonant tones and swore dreadfully. He was subject to attacks of gout, and when one of these occurred, he swore even more vociferously. One day a bull escaped from its corral, and most of the Captain's laborers were engaged in chasing it. When he came upon the scene, the bull ran around a haystack, the throng in pursuit. The Captain, with comments both forceful and profane as to the stupidity of men in general and farm laborers in particular, and condemning their lack of sense and initiative, joined in the pursuit. However, he charted his course in an opposite direction and caught the bull, or rather he met it, head on, at the first corner.

Captain Rabbit had a pony which had been a good pony until it was subjected to his amateur horsemanship when it developed a habit of running away. He drove the pony attached to a cart when he went to town or to market. Whenever the pony ran away it ran home, which would have been all right had it always taken its master with it. After a number of such happenings, Captain Rabbit got his bearings on the situation. Certainly the Captain was not a man to be outwitted by an ordinary pony. When he next went to the seaport town, a few miles distant, he secured a small anchor which had been used by one of the shrimp-fishing boats. To this he attached a heavy rope such as was used for binding loads of hay; the other end he fastened to the axle of the cart; the rope was coiled in the cart. The Captain started forth. In what he thought was a good spot for staging the trick of bringing the pony suddenly to his senses, he dropped the reins on the pony's back and the animal promptly bolted. Captain Rabbit stood up in the cart and tossed the anchor over to the side of the road where the dirt was soft. The anchor "held" and the rope started to run out of the cart. Captain Rabbit's legs became entangled in the rope and he was dragged out, falling heavily on the hard road.

Captain Rabbit had the thought that money could be made in raising chickens. If he was the first one to entertain this idea, he was certainly not the last. People have been making fortunes for many years— in their minds—by raising chickens. But amateur chicken raisers are prone to overlook the items of "depreciation and obsolesence," factors which work rapidly and unerringly in the short life of a chicken. But the Captain had better support for his experiment than most people who have tried it. He figured the chickens would get most of the food they needed around the barnyard, and at no cost to him. Incubators had not yet been invented, and the sunshine in East Anglia was not quite hot enough to hatch eggs. It may be that Captain Rabbit was able to trade "fresh" hens for "setters." Unless one is engaged in chicken production, a setting hen would not be much of an asset. By some means he raised a large number of chickens; so far quite a triumph for such an amateur. Captain Rabbit derived much pleasure from watching his chickens grow; he would show his critics a thing or two. A man who could beat around Cape Horn with a ship that would not sail within six points of the wind was not in need of advice on any subject. He decided that by Christmas he could commence marketing some of his flock. However, one day when he was exultingly watching them, it occurred to him that while they were rapidly taking on weight, they were shrinking numerically. That night he counted them and again in the morning to find to his horror that he had lost two dozen during the night. A much less clever man than the Captain could have found the solution. Someone was stealing his chickens. Selecting a position where he could command a view of the roosts and approaches from every direction, he sat up all night waiting for the thief to appear. But thieves who are easily caught spend their time in jails. Thieves who know their business are sometimes caught but they don't walk into traps. Captain Rabbit sat up and watched his chicken houses for three nights and every morning found the tally correct. During his career as a sailor he had learned to get along with but very little sleep but had retired before he was trained to dispense with sleep entirely. On the fourth night he slept soundly and in the morning found he was short another couple of dozen of his precious fowls. He was desperate. Attending the market in the near-by town—his flock was safe in daylight—he told his friends and fellow farmers of his ill luck. One sympathetic friend said he thought he could help him. "I have," he said, "a large and very vicious dog which I can loan you. I'll bring him over." Borrowing a large and vicious dog seemed to Captain Rabbit like inviting trouble of another kind, but the friend brought him over and tied him with a long chain where he could reach most of the chicken house. The friend explained: "If you feed the dog he will soon become friendly toward you and you can handle him." Captain Rabbit went to bed with a feeling of security. Imagine his consternation when he arose in the morning and found that the thief had stolen the dog and had evidently led him off by his ear, for the chain remained.

Next to the Lion but not adjoining was a double dweller cottage in the south end of which lived Grimmer, the journeyman blacksmith who worked for Topping. The Grimmers had several children, one, a boy named Alfred who was about my age. Alfred once gave me an apricot from their tree which was trained on the south side of the house, the finest apricot I ever ate, and I have lived in an apricot-producing country for more than forty years.

The other end of the double dweller was occupied by Minns, the village butcher. Minns also had a large family, all of whom were girls and naturally could not be of much help to their father in slaughtering pigs. He was a genial, popular fellow who spent a good deal of his time, and a proportionate amount of his money, at the Lion. Mr. Minns led a somewhat uncertain existence which his wife and the girls shared. Sometimes he killed a pig for a villager when the animal reached the killing stage. Occasionally when he had some money he bought a pig which he killed and sold to his neighbors, soliciting their orders while the animal was still living. From this source Mother secured the half pig's heads for pea soup, also the pig's fry which we ate with dumplings. But Mr. Minns's principal though uncertain source of income was from the farmers in the neighborhood. If a cow, a pig, or a sheep were taken sick and appeared not likely to recover, Mr. Minns was sent for to avert a natural death. If he arrived before the animal was cold, he could always do a good job of butchering. It would then be his further duty and privilege to load the animal, properly drawn and quartered, on his cart, take it to town, and sell it. This the farmer himself could not do, for suspicion would have been aroused regarding the farmer's suddenly turning butcher. Mr. Minns had his friends among the meat dealers. He could sell a stillborn calf and could have found a market for a skinned donkey—for sausage purposes—had he wished to do so.

A short distance down the road which crossed the highway close to our house lived a very corpulent farmer named Darrow. Mr. Darrow was an inveterate beer drinker and could have been seen any day at the Lion. He was cordially hated in the village for the reason he had on display, leaning against the wall at the entrance to his yard, a man trap. This was in the year 1873 when apparently it was perfectly proper for those who wished to do so to use man traps on their own premises. It may still be so; I have not inquired. Mr. Darrow had an apple orchard. About the time the apples became edible the man trap disappeared, and everyone knew it had been taken to the orchard. It would have caught a man slightly below the knees but would have closed on my buttocks had I been the one to step into it. After the apple harvest the trap was returned to its resting place inside the gate to be a warning for the next ten months to thieves that they stay away from the Darrow orchard. Mr. Darrow, although he had but a small farm, was the first one in our neighborhood to own a threshing machine. He rented it to other farmers, supplying four of the men needed in its operation, the renter contributing the necessary laborers. Previously threshing had been done by flails and to some extent this was continued. To transport his four men to the place where the machine might be temporarily located, Mr. Darrow supplied a small springless cart called a tumbril in which the men rode seated on some straw. It occurred to Mr. Darrow that cheaper transportation could be arranged. He consulted with Topping. The outcome of their consultations was that Mr. Topping suddenly became very busy and at the same time the center of much interest, for he proceeded to build a vehicle quite unique. Four light cart wheels were obtained, a substantial framework constructed, and after much labor, planning, and measuring, the contraption was complete—a sort of four-wheel velocipede or bone shaker on which each man could pedal his weight. The threshing crew who had watched construction with interest mounted their new horse and started for an outlying farm. After making two or three trips they advised Mr. Darrow that they were not looking for anything worse than hard work and would ride the machine no more. As they were the only ones competent to operate the threshing machine, their cart was restored to service.

For the most part coal was the fuel used in our village. Small amounts of wood were available at times and brush fagots were used for heating the brick ovens in which the bread was baked. There were no ranges or cookstoves. An open fireplace served to heat the home and at the same time cook the food. There were hobs on each side of the fireplace where the kettle or pot could be set, close enough to the fire to keep the contents hot. The oven was separate from the fireplace and built with bricks. The brush fire was placed in the oven and the bricks heated to a degree which would bake a batch of bread after the fire had been raked out. Large open chimneys carried off the smoke and also served to ventilate the room. Periodically these chimneys had to be swept, a job which was always performed by a man named Charley Bott, who lived in the small town some four miles distant. Charley would appear at the time the chimneys needed sweeping. He probably kept no books and if he did he would have needed to use white ink on black paper; he kept a record in his mind of when the different chimneys had been swept and a calculation as to when they should be swept again. His charge for sweeping the chimney always included his retaining the soot, and this may possibly have been all the compensation he received. He sold the soot to the farmers around and applied it to the land, preferring no doubt to maintain a complete monopoly in the soot trade. The soot must have had some merit either as a fertilizer or as a disinfectant. I never learned what it was good for other than to provide a living for the Bott family. Mr. Bott was assisted in his work by his daughter Lucy and his half-witted brother named, or at least called, Billy. To me they appeared a most fearsome trio. Charley Bott had some resemblance to the normal; his bustless hipless daughter, attired in a single skirt which draped her skinny knees and extended to her ankles, may have been an embryo beauty, but if so the fact was well concealed under a heavy and permanent coat of soot. She wore a boy's cap, and while the style of her clothes gave no clue to her age, her shape—or rather the lack of it—indicated that she was in her early teens. She was utterly and uncompromisingly black. Her moronic uncle looked even more forbidding. His face usually wore a diabolical sort of grin as though he had caught the world by its tail and did not intend to relax his grip. At times when they were working in the neighborhood, or when they were passing through the village, they would stop at the Lion. They never received anything more than a lukewarm welcome at that hostelry, but as they were not accustomed to being received with any great measure of enthusiasm anywhere they did not notice what others would have regarded as a slight. They would order beer, of which they all appeared to be very fond, and if they stayed at the Lion for "dinner" they would order bread and cheese, about the only food Mr. Crawshay was prepared to furnish unless he invaded his family larder. However, the Botts made no demands for luxuries. Given plenty of beer, there was nothing more in the world that they needed. They held the food in their sooty hands and did not seem to mind the imprints of their hands on the bread. Their lips were very red, and their teeth and eyeballs showed conspicuously white. It was improbable that Lucy had ever had a bath in her life and quite likely had not washed her face for years. They must have slept in the soot to be so completely covered with it. They had a donkey and cart in which to haul the soot, both of which were as black as soot could make them. It was brother Billy Botts's part of the work to climb the inside of the chimney, which he did by buckling his arms and legs against the chimney walls. He carried with him a short-handled stiff brush with which he brushed off in his descent any soot which he had not rubbed off with his arms and legs when climbing up. Lucy and her father put the soot in sacks and loaded it on the cart. Besides their forbidding appearance there were other reasons why they were not made very welcome at the Lion. Mugs which they used invariably had to be washed—a for-

"Given plenty of beer, there was nothing more in the world that they needed."

mality which was not in general practice—and Billy Bott had, for an incompetent, the very unusual characteristic of being better than an average pugilist. He was also addicted to the habit of drinking other people's beer. Entering a barroom he would stride up to a table and pick up any partly emptied mugs of beer and drink the contents. This was sometimes resented but only by those who did not know when they were well off. Billy had all his pockets filled with soot. If any had the temerity to attack him, he would back up while he reached for two handfuls of soot. He was then ready for the charge and made it by throwing the soot in his attacker's face and eyes. The battle was on. Lucy would edge into the foreground with a handful of soot ready for the rare emergency of her uncle's appearing to be getting the worst of the encounter.

Billy was sometimes arrested as a disturber of the peace, but the magistrates, who usually included at least one brewer, found it hard to be severe with a man just because he had drunk too much beer, whether he or someone else had paid for it. On one occasion he started a free-for-all and a near riot at the Lion. Mr. Crawshay who assumed the rôle of peacemaker in the matter was drenched with his own beer and plastered with soot. It took all of Billy's fistic prowess, aided by his brother, who was at least a good second-rate pugilist, and Lucy with a whole bag of soot which she used skillfully and unsparingly, to quell the attackers. Some of the beer mugs were thrown through the windows, and other damage was done. For his part in the fracas Billy was arrested and brought before the magistrates. This time he was awarded the unusual privilege of stating his side of the case. He had on other occasions been fined a small amount or sent to jail for a few days. He gave a voluble explanation of how it all happened, stating that Jenny Cook and another fellow, two people, and a man had "set on him" and that his actions, as also those of his brother and niece, had been purely defensive.

We often read about the Englishman's addiction to "tubbing," as they term bathing. Papers, the publishers of which intend to be humorous, will depict an Englishman in an impenetrable tropical jungle with a pith helmet, a few cases of Crosse and Blackwell's pickles and marmalade, and his tin bathtub. Only one raised in England can appreciate the humor of such a drawing. The marmalade would be there, but the bathtub, never. In our village no tubbing or bathing under any other name was indulged in. It was considered highly detrimental to one's health to get the skin wet. My contemporaries could not have been made to see anything but disaster as following such an experience. If when I was a boy there was a bathtub in the county, I did not know of its location. And certainly the hazard of drowning in one in East Anglia even today would not be expensive to insure against, for bathtubs are far apart and the inclination to use them, at least on the part of the natives, is anything but a habit. There are ancient bathhouses in England erected by the Romans, but had anyone suggested that the Romans established a precedent, they would have been asked: "Well, what happened to the Romans?" Visitors to England are shown these Roman relics, but although at present nearly every small town and village has its antique shops, they have no bathtubs in their collections. At that our village maidens were no doubt just as acceptable for a "necking bout" as would be the nicotine-soaked flapper of today. Their skins may have needed a little of what was then called "scent," but they did not carry the intolerable odor of stale cigarette smoke.

When my wife and I made a most delightful tour of England and Scotland we stopped for a few nights outside London at a large fine hotel. This hotel had what we presumed to be the Royal coat of arms over its entrance and the sign in large gilt letters, "Patronized by Royalty." We inquired as to the bathing conveniences and were told that there was a tub on each of its somewhat extensive floors. Think of plain ordinary travelers using the bath-tub while the Queen stood outside with one of their heavy eight-by-eight bath towels on her arm awaiting her turn. But we were spared the embar-rassment; nor were we often bothered by other guests' trying the door. Perhaps there are many—and they may be right—who still hold to the theory of a dry skin for health. However, bathed or un-bathed, the British are a great people. Lousiness is a quality of dirty clothing and not of an unwashed skin. Our people did not indulge in underwear. Where it was so difficult to keep the family in cloth-ing, it would appear as the limit of recklessness to wear two shirts at one time.

The only knowledge of dentistry in our part of the country when I was a boy was that of "pulling," as extraction was termed. This was done by any chemist, as druggists were called, at a uniform charge of a shilling a tooth.

Sometimes a brewer's wagon bearing our family name and drawn by magnificent horses passed our house. I asked my father if the brewer was a rela-tive. He replied that if he was related to us, he was certainly not any nearer than a sixteenth cousin, and that personally he preferred to think it was much further removed. We had no known relatives on either side of our family and had no record of ever having had any who were other than lower class,

"We now lived in a detached cottage with quite a large garden."

though when I left England in 1891 I had twelve uncles, thirteen aunts, and about one hundred cousins living there.

When I was six years of age our family moved from the place where I was born to another part of the same village. This was quite a change in my young life. I missed the activity which centered around the Lion and the travel on the London highway. I could no longer watch operations in the blacksmith shop. I had half a mile farther to go to school, but there were compensations—plenty of playmates, all of whom I had already met in school. Further, we lived facing the village green or common. On this we played cricket with home-made bats and wickets. I greatly enjoyed this sport. My father provided me with a hoop to trundle to school. He said it would not seem so far if I chased a hoop. His psychology was good. The hour allowed for dinner, however, did not permit me to go home for that meal. I took my dinner with me. My mother did not spring tempting surprises on me every day but always provided exactly the same kind of food in the same quantity. There was nothing to tickle my appetite, which had nevertheless already developed to almost man-size proportions.

In this new location our next-door neighbors— or rather our nearest neighbors, as we now lived in a detached cottage with quite a large garden, and some plum and apple trees—were a family by the name of Irving. Mr. Irving was a thatcher; thatching was a regular trade. Many barns, some cottages, and all the hay and grain stacks had to be thatched. Mr. Irving was usually busy. His eldest son, Clement, helped with the work. They had a donkey and cart to haul their ladders and equipment. Mr. Irving was a nice neighbor; he made the bats and wickets for our cricket games. One of his sons, Ambrose, an agreeable boy, was just my age. Mr. Irving and his son Clement furnished the music at the Methodist chapel. Mr. Irving played a fiddle and Clement a flute. Sometimes they furnished music at the Lion or any other public house when for some unusual occasion it was required. Mr. Irving sometimes got his tunes a bit mixed and would start one in the chapel which should have been played at the Lion. The music was needed at the chapel only to start the tunes as when once the congregation got its stride, a drum could not have been heard and certainly not a fiddle or a flute. When the singers hit some familiar line such as:

Let every kindred, every tribe
On this terrestrial ball,
To Him all majesty ascribe,
And crown Him Lord of all!

they would be quite carried away with their own melody. One of the Gospel songs which was a great favorite with our village Methodists and which probably quite well represented their religious faith and convictions was this one of which the following is a verse:

> *Stop, poor sinner, stop and think*
> *Before you further go,*
> *Stop, or else you'll drop into*
> *The burning lake below.*

I was enrolled as a member of the Methodist Sunday school and also attended the services. While my parents considered the Established Church as the most proper place to worship, they had no particular objection to the chapel and occasionally attended themselves. The preachers were laymen, sometimes one of our own village laborers but usually someone from one of the near-by villages. They would of necessity have to be drawn from within walking distance, for Methodist preachers did not have coachmen who wore silk hats. I enjoyed the Methodist chapel, in particular the lusty singing in which I could join and I did not discover until later that I have no capacity for carrying a tune.

Once a year the chapel gave a tea party. This was a wonderful occasion. Large quantities of bread and butter and cake were provided. Tea was served in the seats of the chapel, the book ledges being used for tables. After tea, everyone adjourned to the village green where the young people engaged in kissing games. The young men with the most bushy beards appeared usually to be the favorites. Games were provided for the children. The women gossiped to their hearts' content, and everybody had an enjoyable time. For some years it had been becoming more common for the women to boast of the number of cups of tea they had drunk. Six, eight, and even ten cups were disposed of. At the first tea party I attended a young matron set a new and for all-time high record by drinking twenty-one cups of tea.

After spending two very happy years in this location, my family moved to the adjoining village. This was the village which was sharing church and school facilities with the place of my birth, and when we moved I was brought within a quarter of a mile of the joint parish school. I think the inducement which prompted this important step in migration was a very trifling increase in my father's wages. Father was an expert horseman and a good worker. He was never out of employment and commanded what were considered at that time the highest wages. Many people might hold a different opinion about fifteen shillings a week being good wages but it was twenty per cent more than most laborers received, and Father's job was steady. Horses must be fed every day.

I now had plenty of time to go home for dinner from the school, but there was a sad dearth of playmates and nothing of interest near our new home. I had time on my hands. I read a few books when I could borrow any which interested me and sometimes I would visit my father at his work in the fields and walk with him behind the plow for awhile. I think these visits gave my father much pleasure. He would tell me of his life as a boy. He had experienced great hardships in his youth when, after the Crimean War, the price of food had greatly advanced. He told of living for days with frumenty as the only article of food. "Frumenty" is boiled wheat and when cooked in milk or served with sugar and cream may not be a bad dish at all. But the way it was served to Father, cooked in water, and *sans* the sugar and cream, it was nothing but hog feed. Father had an endless repertoire of jokes and stories. We became quite companionable; he treated me as though I were already grown up.

When I was ten years of age, my father made application to the School Board, of which his employer, Mr. Pilcher, was a member, for me to work half time and attend school the other half. The fact that I stood well in my studies may have helped in securing this permission, but the further fact that Mr. Pilcher needed my services may have had even more influence. Permission was given, and I started to work on alternate days. Another boy, Charley Catlin, the son of one of our few neighbors, was given the same permission and worked the days when I attended school. Mr. Pilcher was the only man in the two villages, beside the minister, who could claim to be upper middle class. Mr. Pilcher was a much educated man. He lived in what was known as the Hall, where he probably had his choice of twenty or more bedrooms. He kept four maids, a coachman, a gardener, and had a steward to manage his farm. He held the title of Major from service in the militia; he had been abroad, the only man in the two villages who had had such an experience in the capacity of traveler. Captain Rabbit had been abroad a plenty, but on sailing ships, which were always far behind the liberal schedules allowed them. Besides which, Captain Rabbit probably had but little appreciation of those objects which travelers go "abroad" to view. At heart he was a much finer man than the educated Mr. Pilcher but he was indeed sadly lacking in polish. Jackson, the sailor, had been "abroad" also and had visited many lands but he never knew definitely how he arrived there and could not have given any better account of how he returned. Mr. Pilcher had visited the Holy Land, a trip which in those days was regarded as quite an achievement and one which gave the traveler a sort of inside track to a much desired goal.

Mr. Pilcher made occasional trips to London, the only man in the neighborhood to do so. Beside being on the School Board, he was a magistrate and in that capacity was the terror of local poachers, for he held the opinion that next to murder—and not far removed at that—poaching was the most heinous of offences. If Mr. Pilcher was good at anything himself, it was the job of drinking large quantities of beer and wine, and eating a great deal of meat. He invariably wore clothes which were about two sizes too small for him; he was a large and very fat man. He always wore his coat buttoned to the last button and assumed a sort of military carriage, a habit acquired no doubt when he was in the militia. During my life I have met many educated hogs. The property Mr. Pilcher owned was copyhold, and as he was never married it would go to a nephew who occasionally visited the place. He was a harsh and uncompromising employer, who exacted the last effort from his underpaid laborers while he lived in luxury and ease. He arose at nine in the morning and after breakfast would ride forth over his farm on a fine large horse. He spent some time conferring with his steward, who was a good farmer.

I received one shilling and ninepence a week and my partner, Charley Catlin, the same. Our joint pay of three shillings and sixpence a week was probably less than the cost of a single dinner for the glutton who employed us. The steward held what he considered valuable ideas on how to get work out of boys. He would say, "Two boys are half a boy and three boys are no boy at all." In furtherance of this theory, he never allowed the boys, of whom there were four or five employed on the farm, to have any contact with each other. Usually I was put to work alone. One of my tasks in the spring was to keep the crows off freshly planted grainfields. In my patched misfits, I looked the part of a scarecrow all right. As the two children next to me were both girls, my mother did not think it was economy to buy or make anything new for me. I would outgrow it and the girls could not wear it.

I learned a good deal about crows while I was employed keeping them off Mr. Pilcher's grainfields. A crow is quite narrow between the eyes and has a generally unintellectual appearance. But don't let this appearance deceive you. A crow is a very clever bird; in many tests it would put a college professor to shame. For instance, a field of grain is planted, being drilled in rows. The field is then harrowed twice and as this is done in cross fashion, no trace of the drill marks is left. A flock of crows would descend; each crow would place a foot on opposite sides of the (to humans) invisible drill marks, and would walk along digging up grain with his bill almost as fast as the drill planted it. Tell a college professor to hunt for his breakfast under the same conditions and he will at once decide that a crow is indeed an intellectual bird. It was my ten-year-old intelligence which was pitted against whole flocks of these clever and voracious birds. A cunning stunt of crows is to fly very low as they approach a grainfield. They could not be seen on account of the hedges which usually marked the border line of the fields. They would vault over the hedge and commence to dig. Sometimes I had to watch two or three fields and when I finally drove the crows from one field they would alight in another. They had absorbed the theory that the world owed them a living. Sometimes they divided their forces and attacked on two fronts at the same time. They had no regard for Sunday; consequently I worked on Sundays also during crow-scaring season.

I sometimes saw my partner, Charley, at night when he had been working and I had been at school. I would ask him how the crows had behaved. Charley was an imaginative boy who did not always limit himself to exact facts. He reported: "The crows played a new trick on me today."

"What was that?"

"They crawled under the gate in place of coming in over the hedge."

Charley composed what he called a crow song:

> *There you sit and I don't care,*
> *Fill your craws and make no spare.*
> *If old Jack Pilcher hap'd to come,*
> *You must fly, and I must run.*

Had Mr. Pilcher heard that Charley had referred to him as "old Jack Pilcher," he would have been out of a job and probably his father also, for Mr. Pilcher demanded the strictest deference from his juvenile workers, and for that matter, from everyone else.

It would have been quite an easy matter to have exterminated the crows and have done with their depredations forever, but crows were supposed to fill some useful purpose in keeping certain bugs under control and for that reason were regarded with reverence by all except the boys whose duty it was to confine them to a bug and beetle diet.

When at ten I commenced to work half time for Mr. Pilcher, my childhood was practically ended. Before I was twelve I had passed the required grades to permit me to leave school, which I did, and worked full time. Although religious study was the longest lesson of the day in our school, I had also studied arithmetic, reading, and spelling, and had acquired enough knowledge of grammar at that age to correctly parse in my final examination the sentence, "A little acorn from the top of a tall oak fell and grew into a tree." I could not do it now as I have had so much to think about in the years that have passed that a good deal of what I learned in school has now escaped my memory. I have forgotten most of those several chapters of the Proverbs of Solomon, Son of David, King of Israel, which I so painstakingly committed to memory. Their place in my mind has been filled with much less worthy and inspiring knowledge.

Working full time, I earned three shillings and sixpence a week, all of which went into the general fund for the family's support. This three shillings and sixpence a week was more than the cost of my food and clothes. I was wholly self-supporting before I had reached my twelfth birthday. With my father's average earnings of fifteen shillings a week and with six minor children—this definition of minor children would be any child under twelve and in the case of the girls possibly another year—to support for many years, it can easily be computed that the total cost of my raising to the age of twelve had not been more than sixty pounds, or three hundred dollars. This included Mrs. Gosling's services at the time of my birth, my food, clothing, toys, education, recreation, and every other expense incidental to my proper physical and mental development. Certainly my physical development on skim milk, skilly, bread and dumplings was not in the least lacking. I later had plenty of opportunity to test that out. What might have been done for me mentally under more favorable conditions, it is now too late to speculate on. No consideration is here given for medical service, for I never saw a doctor, and no doctor ever saw me in a professional capacity until I had about reached maturity.

I cordially disliked working for Mr. Pilcher, mainly because neither he nor his steward ever expressed a word of appreciation even when I put forth my best efforts, but they frequently censored me for my lack of application. The steward carefully planned the work on the farm so as to keep the boys on jobs where their quicker movements enabled them to accomplish more than a man would, and at one third the cost. During the summer I would work for weeks alone and without change, digging thistles and pulling wild mustard in the growing crops. Today I hate the sight of thistles and wild mustard. At this work I had plenty of opportunity to think and plan my future life. Even at twelve years of age I realized I was not getting off to a very good start and soon I concluded that life somewhere must hold some reward other than scaring crows and digging thistles. I was definitely souring on the job.

Mr. Pilcher, having income other than that realized from the profits of his farm, was inclined to be somewhat speculative at times. At one of the weekly livestock sales he was high bidder on a lot consisting of nine very large raw-boned old bulls. After the purchase they were driven to the Pilcher farm and put in separate small stalls where they were plied with food, and as they had not space sufficient to move they got the maximum of benefit from what they ate. Soon they were as plump and shiny as overfed bulls should be. When Mr. Pilcher thought the public appetite was all set for a feast of bull meat, he ordered them sent to market. This was a walk of about four miles. I was elected to proceed ahead of the herd, to keep them from taking the wrong turns in the road. I did not feel at all flattered by this distinction. I surveyed the elephantine beasts while they were still in their stalls, then provided myself with a thick club to be used if I were put on the defensive. I proceeded down the road to the first—which was near-by—corner. The bulls were released from their stalls and headed in my direction. The pent-up energy of weeks was allowed to expend itself like escaping steam. With tails erect, they approached me—one monster, a dirty white animal, weighing more than a ton, spotted my red hair and at once singled me out as his lifelong enemy. With head twisted at a jaunty angle, he made his charge. This was a little more than I had anticipated or bargained for. True, I had the club but I forgot about it, which may have been just as well. A twelve-year-old boy would not have much chance in stopping a ton of mad bull with a club. I was smitten stiff with terror. My knees knocked together. A chilly perspiration oozed out of my skin. I could not move, but when the sharp short horn of the bull was within a few inches of my last meal of skilly, I suddenly regained self-control and stepping quickly to one side, the bull charged past me. As he did so I swung on him with the club, which split on his ribs. In a few minutes the bulls were "all in," for they had no wind left. It was necessary to get behind them and prod vigorously to make any headway at all. At the auction they were sold separately and not in a herd as when Mr. Pilcher bought them. There was enough meat in one of the huge beasts to fill an average butcher shop.

One day shortly before I left Mr. Pilcher's employ, the steward suddenly remembered or decided that this was the day when a very large old mother pig was to go to market. He hitched up a cart, putting a heavy rope net over it—something like those used by stevedores to keep freight from falling overboard when ships are being loaded or unloaded. He brought the cart around to the pen, where his innocent victim had been confined while putting on the last one or two hundred pounds of fat. He then looked around for help to load her in the cart. It was my ill fortune to come within the range of his vision at that time, and he called me to help him load the pig. The net was wholly unnecessary. That old pig could not have climbed over any obstacle six inches high and certainly could not have climbed over the sides of the cart. She was almost as high as my chin and must have weighed several hundred pounds. The steward must have anticipated a lot of co-operation from the pig—which would indicate that he yet had something to learn about pigs—if he ever thought we could load her in the cart. Not knowing what the steward had in mind for her, and as her contact with men had usually led to something more to eat, the pig was quite docile. She was engineered around till her nose was toward the end of the cart where she awaited the next favor. There was nothing to do now but persuade her to jump in and, failing that, to pick her up and put her in. No use to expect

"The steward directed me to put my hands under the sagging middle of the huge animal."

any help from a pig under such circumstances; pigs are not so reasonable. One hundred pounds of live pig may not actually weigh any more than the same amount of cold dead pig but it is much harder to lift. The steward directed me to put my hands under the sagging middle of the huge animal. He did likewise, taking such a fierce grip on my hands that I could not let go. "Now lift," he said. We lifted. By the time the slack was taken up under the pig's middle I had changed from a stooping to an upright position. "Now lift again," he said. He lifted so hard that he tilted the pig off its feet. She turned on her side with me under her. She was so deliberate in making her recovery that I almost suffocated. Besides her crushing weight, the pig had a most awful smell. The steward did not sense the fact that I was buried under an avalanche of fat pig. I finally struggled from under her but have avoided eating pork from that time.

Mr. Pilcher was fond of shooting. The term "hunting" could not be applied to the sport in which he indulged—that of shooting hand-reared pheasants which had been reared in readiness for the "season." This he did by hatching pheasant eggs under domestic hens. The birds were carefully guarded until "opening day" of the shooting season.

Nearly all the pheasants were shot or scared to death during the first two or three days of the shooting. Mr. Pilcher sent them in pairs with their necks tied together to his friends but never gave any to his employees. To have allowed any of the local people to taste pheasant would have been to create another and permanent hazard to the safety of the birds. Mr. Pilcher was a real sportsman according to his own lights. He would not shoot a bird on the ground. If they could not fly, they had at least to hop before being shot. When they saw a man approaching, they thought they were to be fed as usual, and it was rather underhanded to give them a charge of shot in place of a handful of grain. The day when the "shooting season" opened was to Mr. Pilcher the most important day of the year. His friends would gather together at the Hall, some coming from as far off as London to participate in the sport. Preparations were made as for an elephant hunt. The day was given the semblance of a wild occasion, though the largest wild animal in the county was a hare. Some ladies would be present wearing costumes suitable for walking through the fields—costumes which they probably had had made for the adventure—and some of them carried guns or had men hired to carry them. Mr. Pilcher's laborers were for the day called "beaters." It was their duty to keep the frightened birds from hiding in the grass. Mr. Pilcher had two guns which his gamekeeper carried for him, handing him one when some birds came close enough to make the job of hitting easier than that of missing them. He also did the reloading. When "shooting," Mr. Pilcher wore a special hunting outfit, a sort of two-way Sherlock Holmes style of cap, a jacket, breeches, and a type of leggings called "buskins." Many traditions were observed, one of which was to eat luncheon in the fields even though not a half mile from the house. They also drank great quantities of liquor. This was needed to keep the gunners' nerves steady and their eyes clear. Special delicacies were provided for the luncheon which was carried to the field in wicker hampers. It was a wonderful day. However, the "beaters' " names were not in the pot or hampers; they provided their own luncheons.

There was one poacher in the village who was a "professional." He did nothing but poach. He no doubt caused Mr. Pilcher much unhappiness. He was an athletic young man who always seemed to have plenty of money. He frequented the Lion but drank only moderately. It would have been unwise indeed had he ever indulged in any habit which would have lowered his mental and physical resistance. He had never been arrested, though everybody knew how he made his living. No doubt Mr. Pilcher would have made it quite well worth anyone's while to have brought about his arrest and conviction. He would have received nothing less than the limit had he ever been brought to justice. Mr. Pilcher would have seen to that. He did not drink enough beer to have entitled him to the mercy even of the brewers and from no source could he have summoned any influence which would have helped mitigate his punishment. But while this man daily—or nightly—violated the laws of a country which has never temporized with criminals or law-breakers, he was in no more danger of being arrested than was Mr. Pilcher himself. There were only two people in the two villages who were supposed to be in any sense responsible for, or interested in, his capture: the policeman who patroled the two villages and Mr. Pilcher's gamekeeper, who was the only gamekeeper in the vicinity. The poacher and the policeman were on friendly terms. There is no doubt but that they often met when out on their nightly rounds and discussed the topics of the day; even policemen must have some human contact. A position to leeward of the policeman's house, when dinner was being cooked, would have given some people an idea. But most of the villagers were like Mrs. Gosling in that they preferred to sell their ideas in place of giving them away. The poacher was the fastest runner in that part of the country but he seldom had occasion to depend on his fleetness of foot to keep him out of trouble. When trouble saw that poacher approaching, trouble and not the poacher did the running. Besides, he had other qualifications usually associated with athletes. Even Billy Bott knew better than to help the poacher drink his beer, and Billy had the reputation of never picking his adversary. Nothing was more remote than that the poacher would meet the gamekeeper when out on his nightly cruises. The gamekeeper took care of that. He had an easy job for which he was paid eighteen shillings a week; this was more than he could have earned by hard work. To have met that poacher alone in a country lane at night would have meant for the gamekeeper, as a minimum of misfortune, a severe beating and temporary incapacity; as a maximum, the loss of his life. The poacher kept two large dogs of the lurcher breed. A lurcher is a special breed of dog developed no doubt by those who needed such dogs, and poachers needed them worse than anyone else. They were of the greyhound type but with longer hair. A greyhound chases its prey holding its nose to the ground and depending on its sense of smell in following the quarry. When a hare was hard pressed it would double quickly. The greyhound could not make these hairpin curves and would drop the scent which it must find again before continuing the pursuit. If the hare could get on a good smooth highway, the chase, insofar as the greyhound or anything else was concerned, was finished in favor of the hare. No other living animal can outrun a hare if the hare is allowed to select the course. The lurcher dog was not the sporting animal that the greyhound was. His sense of smell was equally good, and he used it until he saw the hare, after which he relied on his eyesight. The time the hare spent in doubling in his tracks to escape the lurcher was so much time wasted. The lurcher did not make the bends and curves but went direct for its prey, which it would bring and lay at its master's feet. Another mean advantage that the lurcher used was that, while the greyhound bayed when on scent, the lurcher did its running in silence. Anyone who wished to do so might keep lurcher dogs; no denying any man that privilege. If he were caught poaching, his lurcher dogs would not be of any help in establishing an alibi; in fact they might be used to prove his evil designs.

While pheasants and hares were the most prized rewards of our poacher's nightly endeavors, and he could always "anticipate" the season by a few days, still anything that came to his net might be considered as fish. He had probably known the chickens in Captain Rabbit's flock by their first names and, as for being intimidated by the presence of a "large and vicious dog," he had long before learned the dog countersign and could be sure of a welcome from the worst-disposed of that species. If hard pressed he would not have been adverse to carrying home a lamb, although on account of their squealing habits he would have to pass up the pigs. When apples were needed he may have given preference to orchards other than Darrow's with its waiting man trap.

One of the smaller landowners had a meadow which produced large crops of mushrooms. Mushrooms are a marketable commodity and, unless it is very dark, can be picked with some success at night. The proprietor of the meadow became suspicious that his mushrooms were being poached on. He hid himself and discovered to his surprise that the poacher in this case was a woman. The next night he planned her capture. Three of his men were directed to lie in wait at strategic points around the meadow. He decided on a position for himself where he could, by signal, command the charge. The poacher, who probably had a busy night before her, was on the job when they arrived picking the mushrooms into a clothesbasket. They started to close in on her when, sensing trouble approaching, she picked up her clothesbasket and ran. The watchers made a dash knowing they would catch her when she stopped to open the gate. They were much surprised when the woman, encountering that barrier, leaped over it with her clothesbasket full of mushrooms in her arms. It was our friend the poacher wearing one of his wife's three or four skirts. Everybody knew that there was but one man in England who could jump a five-barred gate wearing a skirt to his heels and carrying a clothesbasket filled with mushrooms, but while circumstantial evidence was strongly against him, the poacher and the mushrooms had both disappeared, which disposed of the matter. The doctrine that every man's house is his castle is of English origin. This worth-while tradition was well known and fully endorsed by this wily poacher, who was equipped with a shotgun, two large dogs and more than the average of physical ability and personal courage to maintain it. English courts are usually very competent in analyzing facts but are extremely wary of hypothetical cases and indirect evidence. No arrests were made.

Mr. Pilcher's gamekeeper kept two large dogs but not of the lurcher species. These dogs were usually confined in small yards with high iron fences. If anyone approached their kennels or yards they would act as though nothing but the fence kept them from tearing the visitor to pieces. When at liberty one of the dogs was a mild harmless animal, but the other was a mean brute. When a puppy he had been teased purposely to make him vicious. Usually his master carried a short leash which he slipped on his collar when anyone approached. One day my father passed close to the gamekeeper, and the dog made a lunge at him. Father was told to keep out of the dog's reach as he knew he would bite and would have no one but himself to blame if that happened. Father did not relish the advice any more than he did the experience but waited until he knew that the dog's master was too far away to render any assistance. He then took a short stick and entering the dog's cage he closed the gate behind him and gave the dog a severe beating. After that the gamekeeper never could understand why the dog on which he relied for protection would howl and run whenever Father came in sight.

An amusing experience happened to me just before I left Mr. Pilcher's employ. He had a great many pigs; raising those animals was his specialty. Mr. Pilcher made beer, or had it made, on his premises. He was much freer with his beer than with his money, but as I did not like beer this helped not at all in my case. Once a large brew of beer went wrong with Mr. Pilcher. Many of the villagers could have told him all about why this happened. The phase of the moon or some other potent influence had been left out of the calculation. Mr. Pilcher, being an educated man, would scorn to consider any such natural influences and he certainly had no respect for village opinions generally. He had been to the Holy Land and had not returned to be taught the ways of life by a lot of ignorant people, most of whom could not have pointed a finger in the direction of the Holy Land. To avoid a one hundred per cent loss, Mr. Pilcher ordered the beer to be given to the pigs. He held the opinion, which most people had at that time, and still have, that anything a pig will eat or drink will make it fat, but I still have my doubts about sour beer being a fat producer. My opinion on the subject was not asked, but I was deputized to carry the beer from the cellar to the large hog corral close by, but not so close but that I had a big job to perform. I was provided with two pails and a hoop, the hoop to lie on top of the pails so they would not swing against my legs. I could walk inside the hoop. When I arrived with the first pails of beer the pigs gave me a most cordial welcome. I poured the beer into their troughs, and they lapped it up. Every time I returned they were ready for more, but after a few barrels had been emptied the pigs began to show the effects of this unaccustomed indulgence. At first they walked in an erratic manner but as long as they could reach the troughs they kept on drinking. After awhile the last pig had given up. There were father pigs, mother pigs, and pigs of all sizes and ages. They lay around in very unusual and most undignified postures, some on their backs with their feet in the air. I continued to carry them beer, filling all their troughs, ready for the time when they could again show appreciation. Next morning they probably all had splitting head-aches and were ready to sign the pledge had they been given an opportunity to do so.

I borrowed and read *Robinson Crusoe*, some of Captain Marryat's stories, and other such disturbing literature. My three brothers older than I had left home and gone on the fishing smacks out of Yarmouth and Lowestoft. My brothers did not give very glowing reports of life on the fishing smacks, but I knew they made much more money than could be made working for Mr. Pilcher. Not much was ever said about the hardships of their lives. They could not be lightened by talking about them, and anyway we regarded a certain amount of hardship as being part of the regular order of existence and never quarreled with the fates. Three shillings and sixpence a week was no great amount to risk in the search for something more remunerative. One might do worse, but not much worse, by surrendering such a job. I decided that I too would go to sea and told my parents of my decision. My father said he did not blame me for being dissatisfied; that he could not see much of a future for me unless I could get into something. He would have liked to have me learn a trade, but this would mean working several years without pay as an apprentice, and, besides, there were no trades in the village other than those of Forman the carpenter and Topping the black-smith, neither of whom employed apprentices, Forman for the very good reason that he had several sons who were in training as carpenters and coffin-makers. My father asked me, for I was still so young to wait another year before leaving home. He told Mr. Pilcher that I was intending to leave, and that worthy gentleman suggested a salary increase of sixpence a week—about the price of a bottle of stout, which he probably thought he was sacrificing. I was receiving only three shillings and sixpence a week, the same scale on which I had started work at ten. Mr. Pilcher regarded boys as boys and did not consider that a boy of thirteen was worth any more to scare crows than one who was only ten years old. The offer of this trifling increase did not flatter me in the least, nor did it greatly relieve the feeling that Mr. Pilcher was taking advantage of me on account of my own and my family's defenceless condition. However, I was not disposed to be too insistent about leaving a home which meant everything that the term "home" could convey. My parents were kind and indulgent; my father had long treated me as though I were already a man and in every sense his equal. I dropped the matter for the time and was greatly surprised when I found a few days later that my father had communicated with my oldest brother Tom and had had him secure me a berth on one of the fishing boats.

For this, my first voyage, I was outfitted almost entirely with articles of clothing which my older brothers gave me. They were woollen and had shrunk to somewhere near my size. Tom gave me a small sum of money, took me to Lowestoft and placed me on board my first boat, a small ketch-rigged craft named the *Eclipse*. I had brought my belongings in a burlap sack. My mother had included a package of currant buns which she made especially for me, also a Bible which she enjoined me to read every day. When I parted from my parents they maintained their calm; I managed to leave without a break. They had said "Farewell" to me, the term "Goodbye" being considered unlucky when addressed to sailors. My father said: "My boy, while we have a home, you have one; you will always be welcome when you return. God bless you." I have often read accounts of first leaving home written by those who were competent to explain the mingled feelings of a boy setting forth on his own at an early age. There is a feeling of exultation in the adventure, but there is also one of inexpressible sadness in the thought of being separated from devoted parents and the home, which however humble, means so much to the one who is leaving it.

When I started working for Mr. Pilcher, my childhood was ended; now at thirteen my boyhood was ended. Henceforth I was to associate almost entirely with men and would be my own guardian and keeper. It was four years before I sailed with anyone as young as I was.

My berth was that of cook. The *Eclipse* was bound for the east coast of Scotland to engage in herring fishing and would work out of North Shields, a small port at the mouth of the Tyne. We spent three or four days getting the boat ready for the voyage, bending sails, taking on the fishing gear, salt, and other supplies. During these few days we lived entirely on bread and cheese, which fact did not develop any problems for the new cook. Many boats were preparing for the voyage. When one boat which had a Salvation Army crew was leaving, the local corps of the Army assembled to see her off.

As her brown sails bellied to the breeze and she glided gracefully through the harbor entrance, the crowd sang:

> *The stars from their element are falling,*
> *The moon shall be turned into blood,*
> *For the children of the Lord are returning*
>   *to their God,*
> *Blessed be the name of the Lord.*

The Salvation Army was, I am sure, an active and beneficial influence among the fishermen, but some of their songs were a bit weird. I could not gather much cheer for my first voyage in listening to them sing such dire predictions as, "The stars from their element are falling."

Voyages were never commenced on Fridays, not because the fishermen were superstitious; no, indeed, but it always happened without prearrangement that no boats were ever ready to start a new voyage on Friday. The provisions were the last thing to come on board. These were placed in lockers, or small cupboards, provided in otherwise unuseable small parts of the boat. The skipper of the *Eclipse* had delegated a young man whom he called Lucifer to instruct me in my work. I was told that I alone was responsible for the provisions and the length of time they were to last. Our list of provisions was not what would be considered passable in a relief camp and would, if served to prisoners in American jails, soon bring on a hunger strike or start a jail break.

"As her brown sails bellied to the breeze and she glided gracefully
through the harbor entrance."

The list comprised salt beef—a long story could be written about the merits and demerits of salt beef—some kind of lard substitute which, while a pale grey on top of the three-gallon pail which contained it, was almost black in the bottom, presumably rendered from packing house offal, but, on the theory that anything can be purified by heat, was no doubt harmless and served the purpose of more expensive fat. This was to be used for frying fish. There were pieces of fat meat which the butcher termed suet, flour, sugar, tea, treacle, baking powder, sea biscuits, margarine, vinegar, pepper, salt, and raisins for plum puddings on Sundays. These fifteen articles and nothing else comprised our list of provisions and groceries. I learned later that some boats had condensed milk to put in the tea, but the crew of the *Eclipse* was not provided with that luxury. Also, by later experience, I found that some boats had soda as a part of their supplies. This the cook could use in hot water to clean the lockers and floor.

Under Lucifer's tuition I learned how to scrub the lockers and floors with short pieces of dogfish, many of which would become entangled in the nets. Dogfish have rough skins which are fine for scouring; also a dogfish is conveniently constructed for that service. I would cut the fish—which are almost round—into sections and when I had worn the rough surface from one piece, would take another. I was not asked to economize on the dogfish. Being

(115)

a dogfish is probably not much of a life to lead but being put to such an ignominious use after death would be indeed a sorry fate to contemplate.

It was anticipated that herring would be the major item in our diet, and they were. The men ate enormous quantities of them, as many as fifteen each for breakfast. From the list of groceries described and the addition of the herring, a thirteen-year-old boy with no previous experience and working under the handicap of cooking on a small craft which was seldom on an even keel, was expected to provide appetizing and nourishing meals. With the exception of the bread used while we were outfitting, bread on the *Eclipse* was limited to sea biscuits which anyway, when soaked in hot tea, were quite acceptable. As we had no spoons, the men would "retrieve" the biscuits from their pots of tea by using their unwashed fingers. In later experience I often contacted biscuits containing weevils. Probably the biscuits had been in stock for some time, before being delivered to the "ultimate consumer." They were usually kept in a locker by the side of the stove. Weevils are a marvelous development which at the time did not impress me at all. They are small brown insects which are produced directly from the biscuits, with no eggs to start with, no bees to effect pollination, isolated on boats or ships far from land —a complete creation. A staggering thought. The weevils were gifted with some reasoning power, not instinct, for they had no progenitors. When the biscuits were dipped in the hot tea they would leave their comfortable homes in the interior of the biscuits and come to the surface in the mug of tea. They did not dive to the bottom of the mug to find a way out. The men would skim them from the tea and a fractional percentage of them may have escaped with their lives to the cabin floor and back to the biscuit locker. The utensils for use in the preparation of the meals consisted of one large convex boiler, one two-gallon teakettle, one very thick and heavy cast iron frying pan, two dishpans, a few large yellow mugs very thick, and an equal number of thick yellow dishes about two inches deep—this for safety when weather was rough. Each member of the crew provided his own knife and fork. We never had any food which required a spoon in eating. While the men had knives and forks, they did not use them in eating fish; it was much easier to deal with fishbones by using the fingers. In the six months I served as cook of the *Eclipse*, none of the crew died and none were sick for even one day. I am willing to concede that the crew were a hardy lot of men but feel that proper credit should be given for these, my first culinary efforts.

The *Eclipse* was a boat of twenty-eight tons. Although ketch rigged, she had a lugsail mizzen. The advantage of using the lugger type of mizzen was that two mizzen sails were carried, one of light

(117)

canvas for fine weather; the other, which was in general use, was made of heavy canvas. This smaller mizzen could be reefed to quite small proportions. She had three different-sized jibs, the two not in use being stowed in the forecastle. She had main and mizzen topsails which when not in use were also stowed in the forecastle, and the yards and jiggers were lashed in frames above the rail on the after part of the boat. She also carried a spinnaker which stretched from the masthead to the bowsprit end and aft to nearly amidships. The object of this large spread of sail was to make the market with fresh fish during fine weather. Herring could be salted, but salt fish seldom brought the price of fresh. When the catch was heavy and the surplus had to be salted, the price variation between fresh and salt herring was less. There was at that time an enormous market in England for fresh herring, which when slightly salted could be converted into bloaters and kippers. The hard salted smoked herring which are sold in America as Yarmouth or Cromarty bloaters are not bloaters as the term is understood in England. There they are called red herring and sometimes facetiously termed "Billingsgate pheasants" or "Two eyed steaks."

We duly arrived on the fishing grounds, and life began in real earnest. The nets would be laid out just before dark, and hauling them in usually commenced very early in the morning, often as early as two or three o'clock. This interrupted my sleep. At my age I needed about eight hours of sleep each night but usually got but four or five during the twenty-four hours. Preparing the meals was but a small part of my many duties. To make tea I had only to add to the quantity of leaves that were already in the two-gallon kettle, the amount of tea prescribed as the daily ration. To secure impartial distribution the sugar was added at the same time. It was then brought to the boiling point when it was ready to serve. About once a week I would have to empty the kettle to get rid of the leaves. The first serving of tea after this had been done would have but a slightly amber tint; however, it took on color with each additional boiling. This recipe, which Lucifer had given me, would not produce tea which an afternoon gathering would rave over, but afternoon tea drinkers are not often deep-water fishermen.

Lucifer had given me the necessary lessons in making suet pudding, boiling salt beef, and cooking potatoes with their skins on. One cannot go far wrong cooking such staples; a half-hour's extra boiling does not materially change the texture of a piece of bull's neck which has been in brine for a year or two. Suet pudding can be cooked the necessary two hours for a fair-sized pudding or cooked for four hours without detracting from or adding to its quality—or what is much more apt to be the case—its lack of quality. Potatoes, even with their skins on, cannot be left to boil indefinitely, but they are much less sensitive than when peeled.

One day when we were in the harbor of North Shields Lucifer decided that we should take advantage of the supply of fresh water available. He said to me: "Cook some dumplings today in place of suet pudding; use fresh water." I had been shown how to make dumplings and proceeded to make them on my own account. Everything went fine. I had the dumplings in the boiler when it suddenly occurred to me that I had forgotten the baking powder. As there were but three elements concerned in making dumplings—flour, baking powder and water—it was really quite inexcusable that I should have forgotten one of them. I went and asked Lucifer if putting the baking powder in the water would help correct my oversight. I had often wondered why this young man was called Lucifer but realized when he had grasped the meaning of my remarks that the name Lucifer fitted him better than any other which could have been given him. A dumpling without baking powder is indeed a "sad" article of food.

My biggest job was in connection with hauling in the nets. As the nets were in a continuous string more than a mile in length, the boat hauled to the nets. A heavy rope was attached to the nets at convenient places. This rope was put on the capstan and the boat hauled by turning the capstan, this being done by hand power. My good friend, Mr. William G. Garrood, had not then perfected his now famous steam capstan. Heaving the heavy boat to the nets was a most laborious task, which was made much more so in proportion to the strength of the wind blowing at the time. It was often a steady grind of six or eight hours. I held back on the rope and coiled it in a small square hold in even layers, much the same way that cable is stowed in a cable-laying ship. This had to be done carefully or the rope would foul when running out. If I allowed the rope to slip—or surge—on the capstan, curses and imprecations would ensue. While I was quite a large boy for my age, still I was not strong enough to perform some of my duties properly. My incompetence brought much verbal abuse on me, the men blaming me for keeping a more competent boy out of a berth. The skipper who was not thirty years of age—in fact the whole crew were very young men —was the mildest in his reproaches, but what he said when he offered any criticism stung worse than the curses of all the rest of the crew. During the summer months there are great quantities of medusa or fully developed jellyfish in the North Sea. These have long trailers and are very pretty as they float in the water but they have the quality of stinging like nettles. They became entangled in the nets and ropes. My face, neck, and arms would be splashed with water containing parts of this terrible growth, and when I should have slept I could not do so for the stinging sensation which lasts for hours after contact.

There was no one of near companionable age on the boat. The lack of sleep, the feeling that I had undertaken something which I could not properly perform, the terrible homesickness—I was not troubled with seasickness as very young persons are not usually subject to that inconvenience—all tended to make me thoroughly miserable. I would crawl into my little bunk, which was no larger than a dog kennel and which I had to enter either head or feet first and, fishing out one of my mother's currant buns from among my meager effects, I would eat it and find some relief in tears. I never ate more than one bun at a time and usually only one daily in order to make them last as long as possible. Even when we came into port I did not fare much better. North Shields may be a very attractive place to those who consider it their home, but to me it appeared to be wholly lacking in charm. As I never went beyond the water front I may not have seen all that it had to offer. I was accustomed to green fields and trees, and there were none of these along the docks. Besides, we usually stayed in port only just long enough to land our catch and then returned to sea.

As the herring moved further south in their migration, we shifted our base to Scarborough, and later to Grimsby. At the end of about three months we returned to Lowestoft and made that port the landing place for our catches. By this time I had fairly well mastered my duties and seldom provoked the men's profanity. When we came up to Lowestoft the herring had not yet become very plentiful. It was early in October, a season when the coasts of England are often visited by heavy gales. In the hope of finding some schools of herring our skipper had ventured a long way to the northeastward. One night we had just finished laying out the nets when it was noticed that the barometer was falling rapidly. The crew was called to immediately get in the nets. We were out in the middle of the North Sea in a twenty-eight-ton boat. The wind soon freshened and delayed our getting in the nets. The nets might have been sacrificed but without their weight in the forehold the boat was not well balanced and could not be successfully handled. It was daylight when they were all finally under the hatches. The wind had already increased to a gale. Sail was set with a double reef in the mainsail. Our skipper was anxious to be getting to the westward; the glass had dropped to the lowest point any of the crew had ever seen. There was something terribly ominous about the situation. The men did not swear. That in itself was significant, for never previously had it seemed possible for them to talk without the use of some profanity. None of them ate any of the herring which I had fried for breakfast, a task of great difficulty owing to the tossing of the boat. The mainsail was barely set before it had to be lowered for the third reef and quickly followed by a fourth, which was the last. The sail was now close reefed. Small boats such as the *Eclipse* can be handled in what would be termed smooth water during heavy gales, but not in the open sea. The waves, which rapidly increase in height with a strong gale behind them, make the sailing of such a small craft well-nigh impossible. However, our skipper was not disposed to give up until there was no hope left for getting further to the westward and out of the wholly unprotected position we were then in. The wind was from the N.N.W.; there was nothing between us and the North Pole to break its force. The boat had been tacked with her head to the N.E. while the last reef was taken, the storm jib set, the mizzen and foresail close reefed. This was the minimum of sail to which she could be reduced with the hope of making any headway whatever. When all was in readiness, the foresail was trimmed to leeward, and the *Eclipse* began to gather headway preparatory to tacking to the westward.

Just then a craft was seen through the spray, which already filled the air, coming up under our lee. The "rule of the road" is inexorable. It was the duty of the *Eclipse* to yield the right of way. To do this she was kept off the wind. This caused a temporarily greater pressure on the sails. Under the added strain the leech rope of the mainsail broke, and the sail split. The craft approaching was a large Belgian trawler under close-reefed sails. The men on the Belgian boat, seeing what had happened to us, immediately "bore up" to go under the stern of the *Eclipse*. As she passed quite close to us, the wind on her beam, her sails drenched with spray, she appeared to me as a magnificent spectacle. To my more sea-soned shipmates she no doubt appeared as a Belgian trawler and nothing else. She was evidently a new boat and had all white sails—most of the fishing craft had brown or yellow sails, these colors being caused by the preservative applied to make the can-vas more durable—and she was twice the size of the *Eclipse*. She heeled over on the crest of a big wave as she dashed by us, showing the full length of her keel at the same time. She "came to" after passing us and continued on her course to the westward. She probably held to her course until she found some measure of shelter. We saw no more boats or ships until the following day.

Under ordinary and some extraordinary condi-tions, those who venture to sea have a very limited measure of protection afforded them by the lifeboats which are carried and by other vessels which can sometimes give succor. But in a seething gale one's only hope is in the craft on which they may be sailor or passenger. I have since that time weathered many hard gales, but this was the only one which afforded me more interest than anxiety. After we were under sail and the gale had increased in force, even before the mainsail split, neither profane nor any other language would have been audible. For a short time after the mainsail split, we rode the gale with some ease. She was now hove to, under storm jib, close-reefed foresail and close-reefed mizzen; whatever the elements had to offer, we were now doomed to accept.

While no breakfast had been eaten, I went ahead with preparations for dinner. The usual piece of salt beef, potatoes, and suet pudding were cooked. The gale had accumulated such force that even under the small bits of sail now standing the *Eclipse* was badly listed to leeward. I put chunks of coal under the boiler on the lee side but even then had trouble in keeping it sufficiently upright to retain enough water to cook the pudding. When the dinner was ready, I crawled along under the weather bulwarks—it would have been quite impossible to walk the deck or even stand up without considerable support—to reach the skipper who was leaning on the weather side of the capstan watching each oncoming wave, though he would have been powerless to help in any way had one broken over the boat. I shouted in his ear, "Dinner is ready." He made no sign of recognition of what dinner meant and right then I don't think it meant anything to him. I have

"It was one of the grandest sights I have ever witnessed."

often read of the hearty breakfasts that some con-
demned murderers have eaten on the morning of
their execution. Being hung or facing that situation
imminently may give a man a good appetite, but
the prospect of being drowned under the next big
wave did not promote any pangs of hunger on the
part of the crew of the *Eclipse*. None of the men
ate any dinner although they had had no breakfast.
However, my appetite—because of my ignorance of
the danger we were in—was unaffected. I stood in
the companionway and watched the mighty waves.
It was one of the grandest sights I have ever witnessed, at least at a time when I had any sense of appreciation. I could see only a short distance from the
boat because of her low freeboard and the spray
which filled the air. The sea was streaked with foam,
and when a wave rolled up to form a crest the wind
tore off the crest and scattered it in the form of
spray. It was impossible to look to windward for
more than a moment, for the pressure of the wind
on one's face made it necessary to turn the side or
back of the head to the wind in order to breathe.
At times one or other of the men would descend to
the cabin to look at the barometer, but it was some
time before that instrument gave them any comfort.
Fortunately the wind was not very cold. While during the day it had seemed that it would be impossible
for the wind to blow any harder, still as darkness
closed around the *Eclipse,* the wind increased in

fury to one continuous and deafening roar. We had no lights, and if we had had they could not have been seen a boat's length away and would not have afforded any protection, for any other craft would have been as helpless as was our own.

All of the men stayed on deck though they might as well have been below. Sailors always appear to have a preference for being drowned on deck or by being washed off it rather than drowning peacefully in their bunks. Not even in the cabin could a light be made to burn, and when the men looked at the barometer they did so by the flash of light when a match was struck. After dark as I stood in the companionway watching the motions of the boat, I would see when she rose on the crest of a wave, her masts bending until the lee rigging was blown out in a bow, and the jib and foresail silhouetted against the sky. Then she would plunge into the trough of the sea, and under the shelter of the next oncoming wave would partly regain her keel, only to be again thrown on her beam ends on the crest of the next wave. As I learned when I became more of a sailor, there were several factors other than the stability of the boat's hull, on which our lives were then depending. If she failed to negotiate each of the immense waves which swept toward her, she would have been engulfed and gone down with hull, masts, and sails intact. Had the mizzen split, she would have "payed off"; with the wind on her beam in place of meeting them with her bow, the waves would have come over the side and swamped her. Had the foresail or jib blown away, she would have come up in the wind and gone down stern first. But as the fatalist would argue: "If you are born to be hung you will never be drowned." I know of the fate of but one of those who comprised the crew of the *Eclipse* at that time. This man was skipper of a boat during the World War. His boat struck a floating mine which was charged to sink a warship. The contact blew the small boat and her crew to bits and whether the crew were on deck or in their bunks at the time did not lengthen or contract the term of their lives by even one moment.

About midnight the gale moderated, and I fell asleep. The mate woke me in the morning to prepare breakfast. I came on deck; the sun was shining brightly, the boat rolled lazily on the swells under the three small bits of sail which she had carried through the gale. I looked around. Not a sail or a wreath of smoke anywhere on the horizon. Apparently everything but the *Eclipse* had gone to the bottom. The mate paced the short deck singing a song which must have been of his own composition, for no printer would have dared to have set it in type. The other men came on deck. They greeted each other with vulgar and profane remarks; danger was not so imminent, and they were again feeling normal. Soon a sail was reported, and after awhile a boat under all fine-weather sails, spinnaker, and jigger topsails, bore down to speak to us. Of all the boats on the North Sea it happened to be the one on which my brother Tom was mate. As she glided swiftly by, our skipper asked to be reported "all well," with only a split mainsail. Our men spread the torn sail out to dry; they ate their breakfasts, then later in the day they laid new strands in the leech rope of the mainsail. They mended the slits in the sail with herringbone stitches and put Stockholm tar on the seams to strengthen them.

Before night we were on our way bound for port. Slowly stemming the outgoing tide, we entered Lowestoft harbor under full sail the second morning. It was a beautiful day but a sad one for many. We had passed many boats outward bound. Work must be carried on; herring must be caught if there was to be a payday. Every flag in town was at half-mast, for already it was known that a great many lives had been lost. The south pier was crowded with people, many women among them, hoping to hear from some boat not yet reported. They shouted the names of the boats they were looking for. Our skipper answered that we were far to the north and east and away from most other boats. He could have told them with a sad measure of accuracy that anything that was behind us would never return. Many boats were lost with their entire crews, and

"Of all the boats on the North Sea it happened to be the one on which
my brother Tom was mate."

others had lost men who had been washed from the decks. The gale was always referred to as the "October Gale." These fishing boats were marvels of construction. The *Eclipse* was built of oak lined with oak, with copper bolts through her outer planking, her timbers, and the lining, and clinched on the inside. The great danger with such small craft and that which accounted for the loss of so many was that they are swamped and carried down under a large wave.

Shortly after we berthed I went on shore to order what was needed to replenish our short list of provisions in readiness for the next trip. As I stepped on shore the owner of the boat, who was the skipper's father-in-law, was standing by. He spoke to me, remarking: "So you are the boy who cooked dinner in the gale." While the skipper had not noticed me when I told him dinner was ready, he had remembered and had told the owner. Whether or not I was a good cook, I am sure no one ever cooked a meal under more difficult circumstances than I had done.

We continued fishing for herring until a few days before Christmas, when the fish which are migratory had disappeared. We concluded our voyage and were paid off. I received more than twelve pounds, which was in addition to my board and the occupancy of the little bunk which had been my berth. This, for six months' work, was more than the amount Mr. Pilcher would have paid me for a year. It was a good earning for one as young and green at that. When we received our pay the skipper passed his cap among the men with the remark, "I think we should give this good boy a little present." He added generously to the amount he had collected and gave it to me. Patting me on the head, he said: "You are the best boy I have ever seen in my life." I had at the outset been a great trial and disappointment to this fine young skipper and was indeed happy to feel that I had made good in his eyes.

I spent Christmas at home with my parents, gave them a part of what I had earned, bought some new clothes—perhaps the first really new clothes I had ever had—and saved a small part of the balance. Since that time I have never been broke.

After a short time I found a berth on a lugger-rigged boat named the *Bonnie Kate* and sailed for the south coast of Ireland to engage in mackerel fishing. The *Bonnie Kate* had a steam capstan which made the work of handling the nets much easier. Nevertheless, it was a dreary experience. We never berthed at a dock but rode at anchor in the bay, usually landing our catches at Kinsale. We fished —weather permitting—seven days a week, which fact irritated the local Irish fishermen. They were too good Catholics to work on Sundays and very much resented our doing so as this tended to keep the market constantly supplied and prices depressed. To go on shore after dark was to invite violence and the probability of being thrown in the harbor. We sometimes landed on the opposite shore of the bay and rambled about the country. The people we met, who were mostly engaged in farming, were friendly, but we found it difficult to hold intercourse with them on account of their and our own pronounced brogues. We spent a good deal of time riding at anchor in sheltered bays and harbors of the coast. We could not fish when the weather was stormy, which was the case a good part of the time.

I was unpopular with the skipper, who regarded me as being too fresh. There was no member of the crew less than about ten years my senior. I had no books to read. One of the men, who could not write, had a girl at home. He got me to read and write his letters but he insisted on dictating every word. I could have done a better job for him had he allowed me to use my own imagination. He invariably started the letter with the remark, "I take my pen in hand." He was very mushy in his correspondence but unless he could do a lot better in person than he ever did in his letters he was fortunate if he ever landed the girl. Her letters to him, which she apparently wrote herself, showed much better style.

After twelve weeks we returned to Lowestoft, and the skipper did not take up any collection as a present to me; he probably would have enjoyed giving me a good thrashing, but as I had never been bashful about mentioning the pugilistic qualities of my older brothers, he restrained himself from committing any act of violence. He did not know any of my brothers and did not wish to make their acquaintance under unfavorable circumstances. Boys, however, mean though they might be, could usually find even among their own crew someone who was ready to play the part of defender.

For this voyage of twelve weeks I received some six or seven pounds as my share of the earnings. I was glad to escape from the *Bonnie Kate*.

After a brief visit to my home, I shipped as one of the deck crew on a large and very fine boat to again engage in the herring fishing on the North Sea. The skipper was a young man with a sullen, taciturn disposition. He had a most capable and efficient crew—with the exception of myself—and why he ever took on such a boy as part of his crew I do not know. He could easily have secured a capable young man for the berth to which he assigned me. Although he had such a fine lot of men for his crew, they apparently fell far short of his ideals. He constantly cursed them both collectively and individually. He was a fine sailor and a very successful fisherman, which fact explained why he had one of the finest boats sailing out of the port and also gave him his choice in selecting a crew which, on account of his overbearing manner and total lack of consideration for their comfort and welfare, he had to do on every voyage he commenced. As the crew worked on a percentage basis, they would not leave after the voyage was started or they would leave behind their accumulated earnings. The rest of the crew, other than the skipper, were a really jolly crowd. It was summertime. I found the life more agreeable than during the previous summer when I had been cook on the *Eclipse*. The men might have complained about having such a young boy in the deck crew, but none of them cared to criticise anything the skipper did or had done.

When we were in port, they went on shore in a body if there was time to drink any beer. The skipper did not go with them, and as I did not like the taste of beer I seldom joined them. They drank a great deal of beer and very rarely paid for any of it themselves. One of our crew, a young man named Garston, was a very fast runner. Foot racing at that time was a popular sport in England. The men would enter a pub, and one of them would let the fact that we had a champion runner in our crew be known to the proprietor. Landlords of pubs were alert in arranging bets to be paid in beer. The information that there was a fisherman clad in heavy woollens who had lacked all opportunity to keep in training, but who was willing to run a race with a half barrel of beer as the stake, was received with joy by the local Nurmis. They would bring in their man, and when our Joe Garston was put forward as his opponent they would want to change the "stake" from a half to a full barrel of beer. They were always accommodated. Joe's backers always stipulated that they have, as it were, the "choice of weapons." The landsmen, with a feeling of shame that they were taking a barrel of beer from some entirely helpless men, would yield anything. A hundred-yard dash up the steepest hill in the neighborhood was decided upon. Joe was good only where his powerful legs and muscles dominated the situation. He always won, after which the crowd returned to the pub, and all drank free beer as long as the barrel lasted. The next day we would again be at sea, and the men would review their previous evening's entertainment with roars of laughter and devise plans for visiting some other pub where they would not be recognized and winning more free beer.

In spite of the skipper's unappealing disposition, I stayed with him for two or three years. When we had finished our North Sea herring fishing voyage, he took charge of a deep-sea trawler, and I went with him. He was equally proficient in either branch of the dissimilar lines of work. For no reason that I ever discovered, he treated me with great consideration; he never swore at me nor criticised anything I did but, on the other hand, tried to teach me some of the many things a deep-sea trawler needs to know. Deep-sea trawling in the early eighties when all the craft engaged in it were sailing boats was about as hard a life as one could select. Boats engaged in herring and mackerel fishing were from twenty-five to forty tons. Trawlers were from forty-five to seventy tons. The boats engaged in trawling—although so much larger—carried out of Yarmouth a crew of six, but out of Lowestoft only five. I know of no life so well suited to develop endurance and the disregard of bodily comfort as that of a deep-sea trawler in those days. The herring boats carried seven or eight in their crews, the larger crew being necessary to handle the nets. The herring boats could not work except in reasonably fair weather; strong winds were necessary to curtail the operations on a trawler, and when she could not work she hove to and awaited a more favorable opportunity.

I was at this time living at Lowestoft, if being on shore one night in two or three weeks or when working at the fleets—one week in eight or nine—

could be called living anywhere but at sea. During the winter months the life was one of unmitigated hardship. A great deal of knowledge and experience was necessary to become a successful trawler. Seamanship in handling the trawler, skill in handling an open boat in a rough sea, a knowledge of the fishing grounds, skill in mending nets and gutting fish, were all requirements of a competent trawler.

We are all born with opportunity to excel at something, and certainly my opportunities were far greater than those of the average man. At gutting fish I soon became an expert. I never excelled at anything else in my life but at gutting fish I was the "unbeatable champion." Truly, not an accomplishment which would advance me very rapidly in the direction of lower middle, upper middle, or any other higher social class, and certainly nothing to boast of in polite drawing room society. Still, fish must be gutted; no one would wish to eat even the choicest species unless they had undergone that essential operation, and I can still think of many things much more repugnant than that of dressing a nice fresh fish. I could attack a deckful of fish, gut the fish, toss them to the other side of the boat, keeping one constantly in the air. If you think this cannot be done, go to Yarmouth in November and watch the Scotch girls—working in brine in the open air on a frosty morning—gutting herring. Nice girls well qualified to be the mothers of the next generation. Makers of an indifferent quality of beer are often knighted—perhaps for not making it any worse than they did, while it was in their power to do so—but champion fish gutters are never knighted nor even given "honorable mention."

During the summer months trawlers were often formed into fleets. When the weather was fine the clumsy heavy boats would lose so much time going to port with their individual catches that small fleets were formed and some of the trawlers supplied with ice for the conservation of the fish. The others would transfer their catch of the night to the one assigned for the run. This arrangement kept most of the boats at sea for several weeks at a time. The boats engaged in the carrying would be designated as "cutters." Others joined the large fleets operated by London fish firms which had small fast steamers for cutters, one leaving the fleet for London direct every morning. These fleets were in operation all the year, but the number of vessels at each fleet was greater in the summertime. I was one of the crew of a trawler out of Yarmouth at one time and was stationed with Lulu and Morgan's fleet, otherwise known as the "short blue fleet," for each trawler carried a short blue pennant. However, this fleet at the time I was with it was more familiarly known as the "duffers" fleet, this for the reason that many of the men forming the crews of the trawlers had been with the fleet for most of their lives. Spending almost all their time at sea with a small crew of ignorant men and no social or cultural influence whatever, often drinking for the few days they would be in port, the term "duffers" most aptly described them. At that the pay was small, the hardships most severe, especially during the winter months, and, added to all that, the loss of life was very heavy. Not a large number of the boats were lost. They were built to withstand the weather, but many lives were lost in ferrying fish to the cutters in open boats, and frequently men were washed overboard from the low hulls of the trawlers.

The large fleets were under the leadership of an admiral, and usually the fastest trawler in the fleet was selected to carry his flag. He would be a man who had been successful and possibly a little above the average in intelligence, which fact would not necessarily place him in the "wonder" class. All the movements of the fleet synchronized with those of the admiral and were directed by flags during the day and a system of rockets by night. Owing to the great loss of life, Parliament at one time passed a law obliging each trawler to be equipped with life preservers, which the boat crew had to wear when they "boarded fish." The men found the life preservers, which were the ordinary cork jacket type, so hampered their movements that they refused to wear them. Once when I was with the "duffers" fleet the admiral hoisted the flag for "boarding" when the wind was blowing a near gale. A son of the skipper was one of our boat crew. Of the crew of six, three would go in the boat with the fish to the cutter, the skipper, mate, and cook staying with the trawler which would be run to leeward of the cutter and hove to until we again came on board. This may have been the reason why six was the usual crew out of Yarmouth. As they worked with the fleets more consistently, in ferrying fish from Lowestoft trawlers, only two would go in the boat. On this occasion the skipper, seeing his son's life placed in jeopardy, stated he would throw the catch of the night overboard rather than risk the men's lives in making the transfer. As no ice was carried, the fish would not have much value on the following day. The skipper's son, however, promptly told him not to heave any fish overboard on his account as he did not wish to show the white feather and was prepared to perform his duty and carry out the admiral's orders. It was then decided that the transfer should be made. Neither the other member of the boat's crew nor I were asked how we felt about it. We successfully accomplished the difficult task, but never before nor since have I been in an open boat in such a sea. It was a bit of foolhardiness, and the admiral was drunk or crazy to give such an order. So few obeyed him that the cutter did not have enough fish to justify making the run and stayed with the fleet.

It might not be expected that discipline and obedience to commands would be very closely observed by a few ignorant men on a fishing smack. Still, the "willingness to obey"—although probably no one in the fleet could have written a thesis on the principle—was quite generally understood as being primary to a "fitness to command." The skippers were not bound to accept the admiral's orders in a matter pertaining to the safety and personal welfare of the crews for whom they were responsible. It, however, appeared to be the admiral's responsibility to keep everyone in the fleet working day and night. When there was no wind his plans would not work, but when there was wind, there was plenty of action, shifting to new fishing grounds, regaining positions lost while dragging the trawl. With his faster vessel he could keep the slow ones doing their uttermost not to lose sight of the fleet or get so far to leeward that they could not put their fish on board the cutter. This meant a great deal of work in setting, shortening, and trimming sails.

At this time there were more than two hundred trawlers at the "duffers" fleet. With these large fleets there would usually be one or more "copers," or floating rum shops. These were of Dutch or French registry. They were usually trawlers which

"It was at this time my good friend, Doctor Wilfred T. Grenfell, appeared on the scene with his Mission to Deep Sea Fishermen."

had been acquired and refitted for the purpose. Tobacco, which in England was very heavily taxed, was sold at a price far below that at which it could be bought in the home port. They also sold liquor and perfumery. They sold many small articles of French manufacture which were subject to heavy duty if landed in England. They also sold obscene playing cards which looked like ordinary playing cards—and which could not have been sold or given away in England except at the vendor's risk—but when held before a light, revealed pictures which only a Frenchman could think of. During fine weather they did a large business with the crews of the trawlers, but men often got drunk on their potent firewater, and loss of life sometimes resulted in returning to their vessels.

It was at this time my good friend, Doctor Wilfred T. Grenfell, appeared on the scene with his Mission to Deep Sea Fishermen. Doctor Grenfell had visited the fleet on one of the steam cutters and saw the great need for the betterment of the conditions under which the men at the fleet lived and worked. The first of the Mission ships to arrive were reconditioned trawlers, but later, as Doctor Grenfell was able to arouse interest in his work, fine new vessels considerably larger than the trawlers were entered in the service. Later he was able to secure permission from the Government to sell tobacco without paying duty on it. As the sale of tobacco was the principal article of the "copers" trade, the loss of this business drove them off the sea, taking their rum, gin, and perfumery with them. Doctor Grenfell, who has become famous first through his Mission to Deep Sea Fishermen and later by his work among the fishermen of the Labrador coast, has written several books which I can recommend to anyone who is interested in learning the amount of real benefit and usefulness one man can render his fellow men during a lifetime of self-sacrifice and devotion.

On one of my infrequent visits to port I had an opportunity to ship as a sailor on a small steamer bound for America. The life of a deep-sea trawler was not so alluring but that I thought a short time could be spared for experimenting in other lines, beside which, there was a fascination about the very word "America." I had never heard nor had I read much about that great country but what little I had learned had given me the idea that America was not only a land of freedom but also a country of easily acquired wealth. I did not tell anyone of my intention, which was to run away from the ship as soon as she touched America's shores. Boston was the steamer's destination. I knew no more about Boston than the average Bostonian knew about life at the "duffers" fleet, which is, I am sure, an admission of but little knowledge of the famous New England port. I found out during the voyage, without revealing my purpose, that running away from English ships in American ports was not actively encouraged by those who were responsible for the steamer's schedule. However, I kept my own counsel until the evening after we landed, at which time I had an opportunity to go on shore. The prospect for a getaway did not look so promising unless I wished to go ashore with only what I stood in. The dock was enclosed with high gates which were closely attended by an uncompromising-looking watchman, whose duty I surmised was that of thwarting the carefully laid plans of would-be runaways or to at least do his best, and I concluded that most likely he had working arrangements with the police. I passed through the gate unchallenged and started my search for a "hide-out" where I might secrete at least a part of my belongings. I selected the Enniskillen House, a small frame structure on Marginal Street, East Boston. It was a longshoremen's boardinghouse. The landlady was a young and very pretty Irish woman. I took her into my confidence with the hope that she would respond to my evident need of a friend and adviser. "Come on shore," she said, "with all the clothes you can wear and return to the ship with as little on as the policeman will allow you to walk the street in." I went back to the ship; all the men had gone ashore. I dressed up and again sauntered leisurely by the watchman. When I had got away from the dock I made better time and reached the Enniskillen House in a state of near collapse from the sweltering heat. The landlady showed me to a room where she said I could "strip" and leave my surplus clothes. I returned to the ship wearing only a jersey and a pair of trousers. The watchman did not notice the difference or at least made no comment. It took me three nights to get my belongings ashore as I did not dare go on shore more than twice in one evening. Had I been questioned, I might have found some excuse for the second trip but I could not have explained a third, and might have been denied permission to go on shore again. At that, the watchman must have been indeed dumb for his kind—who are usually supposed not to be much above the water-front average —or I could not have made so many "loaded out" and "return empty" trips without being noticed. I carried an extra pair of shoes in my hand on one trip as though I were headed for a cobblers. I could manage two pairs of trousers at one dressing but not two pairs of shoes.

When I had everything on shore I told my landlady I was ready to go into residence. She assigned me to a small room and one-half of a double bed, the other half of the bed being the sleeping place of an Irish longshoreman. My landlady advised me to lie low until the steamer left port, stating that such good-looking sailors as I were rare and an effort might be made for my recapture. At dinnertime I met my roommate or, more intimately speaking, my bedfellow who later in the evening suggested that perhaps we might as well go to bed. I was interested in my partner's preparations for bed. He wore shoes, pants, and a knitted garment called a singlet. He removed his shoes and trousers but retained the singlet as a sleeping garment and was then ready for bed. I was sleeping the sleep of the free if not of the just when a noise in the adjoining room awakened both my bed partner and me. Some lodger had come "home" very drunk and was stumbling around in the other room, occasionally breaking forth with a line or two of a song. Apparently he was not exceeding the privileges of the Enniskillen House; with a muttered imprecation my partner settled down for another doze, but was suddenly electrified into motion by a soliloquy emanating from the other room. "I love her as the Lord loves Holy Water," said the drunk. My companion, leaping out of bed, remarked in very good Irish, "The divil be talking about the landlady," and disappeared. I heard through the thin partition the sound of hard fists in contact with a soft head; then all was quiet. My bedmate returned to his bed; we resumed our interrupted slumber.

I kept well out of sight till the steamer left port, for I did not wish to embarrass anyone, least of all myself. Then I started out to look for work and soon found an employment office on an upper floor on Washington Street. The charge for a job was a dollar, and I could sit in the room reserved for applicants until I secured one, but with no guarantee from the agent of when that interesting event would occur. The waiting room was small, with benches, without back supports, on all four sides. The employment agent did not make his clients too comfortable or they might have preferred his waiting room to a job of work. These benches were quite well filled with assorted unemployed—the Irish predominating. They must all have been in earnest to some extent or they would not have paid a dollar for a seat. It was summertime; they could have sat in the parks. People came and went all day. The waiting crowd chewed tobacco. Cigarettes had not yet been invented. When they finished with a chew of tobacco, they threw it at the ceiling endeavoring to stain one of the few spots which had not already been hit. They told each other improbable yarns, but none of them seemed to think very highly of farm work when that line of employment was mentioned. Some were engaged and left; others took their places. On the afternoon of the second day, a tall, thin, and very much sunburned man appeared and, running his eye over the crowd, made straight for me as though he knew a good man at a glance. He asked: "Are you looking for work?" I told him I had sat in that same spot for two days looking for a job. "Can you milk?" I had to admit that I did not know how to milk a cow. My work for Mr. Pilcher had been that of scaring crows—which never stayed scared long at a time—and digging thistles, for the most part. His next question was equally unfavorable. "Can you mow?" No, I couldn't mow but I saw that if I were to sell myself I would have to be alert. I told my inquirer that, while I could neither milk nor mow, I was very anxious to become proficient in both those acts. If manual skill were hereditary, I should probably have been one of the finest milkers and mowers who had ever set foot in Massachusetts. "How much wages do you want?" "Whatever I am worth." There were then, and probably are yet, many men in Massachusetts with whom it would be safe to make such an open contract, but I had not found one of that kind. He closed with me quickly and told me to get my things and meet him at the station. When I arrived at the Enniskillen House and apprised my landlady of my good fortune, she was unable to see the situation in such a favorable light. She begged me not to go on a farm, stating: "They will starve you, besides which, you are welcome to stay here till you find other work." But I paid her for the meals I had eaten and for the half of the bed I had occupied, took my belongings, and went to the depot. My new master had me purchase a ticket to Bedford, which is not New Bedford but a village about five miles beyond Arlington and in or near a somewhat historic neighborhood. However, what I did not know about historic American neighborhoods would have comprised a good many volumes. On the way out my employer told me that I should be located only about three miles from Lexington and four miles from Concord, and he was probably disappointed that I was not more thrilled with the prospect.

We arrived at the farm—the farmer's wife having met us at the station—just before dark. My master said that as there was still some daylight left we could try a few strokes with the scythe at once. A low soft place where the mowing machine could not be run was selected, and I started to swing the scythe. One would not need to travel far to find many men more competent than I ever became at mowing hay, but they would be on a long hunt trying to find more mosquitoes to the square foot than I found in that swamp. They must have been standing on each other's backs for lack of ground space. They arose in clouds but promptly alighted on me, and from the way they stuck it was evident that they had never before found anything quite so tasty as a runaway sailor. Darkness came to my relief. We quit mowing because we could no longer see the grass. My master seemed to be somewhat disappointed in my technique but no doubt he also felt relieved that he did not have a one day-coach fare, Boston to Bedford, invested in such an unpromising employee. He then showed me to my room, a small shack detached from the main dwelling. I was told that milking would commence at four-thirty and to be sure to be on time, for cows were peculiarly sensitive to regular hours and care.

At four-thirty I appeared at the barn but I had not taken my master by surprise unless he had anticipated my arrival a half-hour earlier. He evidently felt it was then too late in the day to wish anyone "good morning." He was apparently a daylight saver, saving it at both ends of the day. There were seven cows. I was shown how to seat myself and get results. My employer stated that the first cow was nearly dry, and I could first practice on her. A cow is a dumb animal—at least in the lexicon of the Society for the Prevention of Cruelty to Animals—but this cow was not so dumb; also she had reasoning power, and she reasoned why, when she was dry, should she be subjected to the humiliation of being "milked." With a dexterous twist of a foot she rolled both me and the stool to one side. I promptly lodged a complaint with her owner. He gave me a new start. Said he: "You tickle the cow; go like this." Soon I had the cow liking it, or by some further process of reasoning she had decided to submit to the indignity. I was better at milking than I ever became at mowing, for there were not so many mosquitoes. Soon all the cows were entrusted to my care at milking time.

Then my master began to coach me in the care

of the horses. There were three of these. "Jawn," he said, "you take care of these two, and I'll look after the colt myself." I told him my name was George, not John, but he insisted: "I always call the hired man Jawn." The first horse was docile, and I thought quite sensible. The second one eyed me in a manner most disconcerting, at least to me. He looked around at me and, being in his stall, was obliged to turn his head at a sharp angle to see me; he showed a great deal of the whites of his eyes. I decided to trade him on the spot. I suggested to my master that he take the second horse, and I would take the colt. I explained that I did not think, from the way in which he looked at me, that the second horse was disposed to be friendly, and I was afraid he would kick me. My master said: "Jawn, a horse cannot kick unless he raises his tail; just hold his tail down and he is helpless." This must have been sound logic. I have never submitted the idea to a horse trainer. I would reach around the stall partition and, grasping the horse's tail, I would swing in on it. I was not kicked and, as for being bitten, I did not curry that end of the horse. There were rats on the farm although what a New England rat lives on would be a problem for a scientist. At night they scampered around my room, but this did not often disturb me. One night, however, an unusually careless rat in running over my face set a foot in my eye. I reported this to my employer, who gave me the comforting assurance that this would not happen very often. "You see, Jawn," he remarked, "it rained last night, and the rats could not go out. I am sure that when the weather is fine you will not often be bothered."

My Irish landlady was right. I was almost starved. Seated with the family at one end of a long table with nothing within my reach, I left the table more hungry than when I sat down. I tried eating apples, which I could get when no one was looking. I even tried cucumbers, but both of these appeared to be appetizers. One day I helped my master pick some green corn, which he later took to Lexington for sale. I had never before seen green corn. I asked him how it was prepared and was told, by husking and boiling. Then I asked if it was good raw. My unsuspecting employer said he had seen men eat it raw. I changed the subject of conversation. When one knows all there is to be known about something, or at least all that "they" need to know, why delve for further information? I never did like to learn too much at one time. Overdoses of wisdom suddenly thrust on one are likely to create a sort of mental indigestion. That night after the family had retired and ostensibly I had done the same thing, I left my bungalow. The family dog was friendly—he did not get any meat to make him vicious—and I had no reason to anticipate trouble from him. He had during his short life seen so many "Jawns" that, like his owner, they had lost all individuality—or never possessed any—and significance to him. I went out to the corn patch where we had picked corn. I could find the ears by feeling up the stems. I had a glorious feast. Carefully burying the stripped cobs I returned to my sleeping quarters. The next morning I beat the cows to the rise. I was dreadfully sick. I think even the dog was sorry for me; if anyone else was, they did no better than the dog in expressing it. If my master had any twinges, they were probably due to his reflection on my temporarily lowered efficiency. I am sure his nerves were well attuned when he had any financial interest at stake. He said: "Jawn, you have the worst case of summer complaint I ever saw." He probably would have liked to have blamed it on overeating—which it was—if he had thought he could convince me that it was. Since that time I have restricted my use of corn to eating corn-meal mush and occasionally corn-meal muffins, leaving the green immature product for the use of those who have never properly tested its potentialities.

At the end of a month, for my best efforts, I was paid eight dollars. As deck hand on a trawler I would have received fourteen. The eight dollars may have been all and more than I was worth, but I had come to America to get rich, which goal I figured I would be a long time in achieving on eight dollars a month. I advised my employer that I was leaving and that, as he had not given me any notice when I entered his employ, I did not feel that it was incumbent on me to give him any when I was leaving. My master went to town on the same train which carried me in but he did not bother to tell me any more about the history of the neighborhood. He was no doubt wondering what success he would have in finding another "Jawn" during what was then the busy season for farmers.

Some forty or more years later my wife was in Boston and went out to Bedford to see the dear people for whom I had worked one month, the seven cows I had milked, and the horse which could not kick unless it raised its tail. But only my former mistress was living and she was living alone in the house which in the meantime had become very much out of repair. I had roamed around risking all manner of poor cooking, some of it my own. My ex-master had stayed on in the peaceful little New England village and had met a violent death caused by a stick of wood hitting him in the head when he was chopping. In the meantime the seven cows had gone permanently dry and had become the prey of the butcher. The three horses had been replaced by other and perhaps more tractable beasts. So impressed was my wife by the mistress' extraordinary recollection of this one particular "Jawn" that when she returned to Boston she wired me at some length that the mistress remembered me and described me most accurately. Hardly telegraphic news, perhaps? After having a new hired man every month for forty years, this might seem a bit unusual but not at all. It is highly improbable that in eighty years she would have met another who was quite as incompetent as I proved to be. A "hired man" who could neither milk nor mow would be a novelty at any time.

I had had the usual excuse for a breakfast before leaving the farm in return for having milked the seven cows and curried all of one horse and the business end of another. I returned to Boston and the Enniskillen House. My pretty landlady was horrified at my appearance. She exclaimed: "I told you that they would starve you. Come and have some breakfast." I had supplemented the Bedford breakfast with a plate of baked beans as soon as I alighted from the train but I could not refuse, she was so genuinely interested in my welfare so I sat down and ate a real breakfast which, it being then long after breakfast time, she had prepared especially for me. I then went out to look for more work. In my wandering I reached Faneuil Hall Market. There was a booth at which edibles were displayed. I had already eaten three breakfasts, one of which was a real meal, but my enfeebled resistance could not withstand the sight of the pastry. I ate a few helpings, after which I sat on the stone steps of the market, having selected this seat because I was too full to move another step or even to stand up.

My former bedfellow welcomed me to half of the bed we had previously shared. All I needed now was a good job. I did not go to the employment office, thinking I would rather seek the job than have the job seek me. I had concluded that jobs which go looking for takers are not apt to be the best kind of jobs. I have never been in politics but I know I possess some of the fundamentals. When you want something, go after it and don't quit till you have it. I had already learned how to provide inexpensive meals, for I had discovered Boston's famous "bean parlors." I spent most of my time on Atlantic Avenue and Commercial Street or along the Boston and East Boston water front. I soon found that baked beans served in restaurants with waitresses wearing black sateen blouses cost fifteen cents. In ordinary longshoremen's restaurants they were ten cents. But I found a place operated by a large negro who wore only a red undershirt and pants. Here beans were five cents. I attribute my small success in merchandising to the fact that I always planned to make my profit when I made the purchase and not when— as most merchants do—I made a sale. I bought my beans from the negro at five cents a plate, which was a one hundred per cent profit when compared to paying ten cents. Bread was included, the science of dietetics not yet having advanced to the point where bread and beans were not regarded as an ideal combination. But there was a trick about this negro's bread piles. A plate of bread, five or six slices, was served with the beans, but only two slices of the bread were edible, the other or foundation slices being so dry and hard that they could not be cracked with the teeth. No check was given with the meal, but the negro collected five cents from each patron as he left somewhat as fares are collected on the overhead and underground railways. That negro did not know it but he was right in the van of American progressiveness. Coffee—there was no choice of beverages—beans, and bread for five cents. Any departure from that with a line of salads and sundaes would have meant a menu card, overhead which could not have been met with a five-cent charge for beans. It is only when one reaches about as far west as the Missouri River that baked beans become "pork and beans." There is no pork in Boston baked beans. Massachusetts is not a hog country; it is a Pilgrim country, and Pilgrims are always seeking places where there is little or nothing to eat. No one could make good as a Pilgrim in a land of plenty.

A neat-looking schooner was moored at one of the docks. I went on board and accosted the only man in sight who appeared as though he might be the captain. To my inquiry as to whether his crew was complete or not, he replied that he was short one sailor. He was probably short a whole crew but con-

"That negro did not know it but he was right in the van of American
progressiveness."

cluded from my youthful appearance that there were some berths I could not qualify for and certainly could not fill two positions of any rank. I was shipped—without much questioning—as an able seaman to sail on the following Thursday and went on shore to idle away the intervening days till the date set for the schooner's departure. This time should have been spent at the public library or in seeing some of Boston's historic features, but I did not leave the vicinity of the water front. I did not have that thirst for knowledge which is properly supposed to fill the minds of the young. In the part of the city where I spent my time I was not exposed to much of the culture for which Boston is—no doubt justly so—famous. I ate breakfast and dinner at the Enniskillen House, rode back and forth across the channel on the penny ferry, ate beans at the negro's for lunch, watched the water-front activities and on the whole was about as well satisfied as a boy at a circus. A day or two prior to the date set for the schooner's sailing, as I wandered along the water front, I was stopped by a runner for a sailor's boardinghouse, who offered me a berth on an English steamer. When I told him I was already shipped and mentioned the schooner's name, he said the captain would have difficulty securing a crew to sail on the date set or on any other near-by date, for he was bound for the "Islands," and the yellow fever was very bad there at the time. His remark had the effect which he no doubt intended. I shipped as one of the steamer's crew and was told to hurry, for her departure was imminent. I got my clothes from the Enniskillen House, paid my bill, and bade my fair landlady goodbye. In 1927 I was spending a few days in Boston. I then tried to locate the Enniskillen House but could find no one who knew where it had stood. I could not find the landlady; in fact, I could not recall her name. I am sure that had I found her she would still have been pretty with her blonde hair and slightly tilted nose. She had lived among rough people and her surroundings generally were not of a very refined order, but her heart was big and it certainly was in the right place. She was an earnest little Catholic and is entitled on her record to canonization. The penny ferry was still in operation. Boston and Lowestoft have something in common.

The ship to which I hurried was a small freight steamer which had just completed her loading, the last consignment being six hundred and fifty Texas cattle as a deck cargo. It was August and fearfully hot. The steamer, a near successor of the *Mayflower,* was of twenty-one hundred tons, this tonnage having been in part created by cutting the ship in halves and adding a considerable section to her middle. Her length—nothing very great at that—was out of all proportion to her beam. In her youthful days, which were long past, she had been an Atlantic pas-

"The ship was rolling in a manner which left no doubt—and required but little calculation as to the time—she would roll over."

senger liner when a ship of one thousand tons was some ship. She had negotiated the storms of the Atlantic for many years and was still on the surface and prepared to render more service. The *Queen Mary*, or the *Normandie*, will not do any more. This old ship had operated to an advantage in developing the United States, in that passengers who came over on her would endure a good deal of hardship in the new land before they would consider a return trip on such a boat. Some of the cattle were "stowed" in improvised pens on the upper deck from where they would have been swept overboard, minus life preservers, had we encountered any heavy weather. But most of the cattle were under the deck in what, at an earlier date, had been select cabin quarters.

As soon as I was on board the ropes were cast off and the steamer dropped away from the dock. None of the cattle had had shipboard experience. The ship rolled gently as she moved from the dock. The cattle braced themselves; she rolled the other way. They again braced for the roll. In a few minutes, owing to the action of the cattle, the ship was rolling in a manner which left no doubt—and required but little calculation as to the time—she would roll over. Orders were given for full speed astern. This enabled the ship to regain her keel, but it shut off all air circulation to the sweltering cattle under the deck. The ventilators had been set with the idea that the ship would proceed bows first toward Liverpool. Having recovered her equilibrium, the boat was turned with her bows to the job in hand. In the meantime the temperature below had mounted to the point where several of the cattle had suffocated. The boatswain's mate, not asking for volunteers, took me with him to the between decks to get out the dead cattle. Space was so limited that there was not room for all the cattle to lie down, dead or otherwise. It was the duty, or one of the duties, of those who tended them to keep them constantly on their feet. If they were allowed to lie down for awhile they could not again be made to stand up. It was great sport working in a temperature which would and had already killed a lot of Texas bulls, but I would not be outdone by any boatswain's mate, whatever the temperature might be. We took a lanyard with us but following the boatswain's lead instead of going down the narrow aisles where the cattle stood head to head, tethered with short halters which prevented their reaching each other across the aisle. The boatswain jumped on the back of the first one and, traveling on all fours, made much faster time than could have been made using the aisles. The cattle snorted and bucked, but by the time one had a good arch to his back we were three or four bulls down the line. To have gone down the aisles would have required that we have short sticks to tap them on the noses as we moved forward. This would make them step back and allow room to pass. They were quite willing, and perhaps anxious, to give anyone a dig with their sharp horns had they been given an opportunity. We traveled singly, however, and when we reached a dead one we made fast the lanyard to a leg or around the neck of the animal, released his halter. The boatswain blew his whistle, and the bulls were hoisted on deck, having been hauled over, under or between those still living. While I reflected on how Minns, our village butcher, would have felt had he been present, we rolled them overboard. As Minns never considered an animal dead until it was cold, he would have felt that these cattle were very much alive and that in throwing them overboard we were drowning good beef. Later, when I had had a chance to try the ship's beef, I felt as badly about it as Minns would have. The smothered cattle should have been kept for the use of the crew. Additional canvas windsails were hoisted to get air to the lower deck, and soon the temperature was reduced to where the cattle had some chance of survival.

Our crew were a mixed lot: only two able seamen of whom I was one—and none too able at that; the other was a large and very black negro, who was instantly friendly. As we were the only two of that class on board, it was essential that we be good friends. I have no race prejudices; I felt just as friendly toward the negro as his manifestations indicated he did toward me. Four ordinary seamen were carried as part of the crew. The ruling making this necessary must have been an early day idea of "spreading the work." The small amount of work necessary to be done on that old steamer would have needed to be well spread if it was to be performed by our ordinary seamen. No doubt it was in compliance with some law that a ship of twenty-one hundred tons should carry six seamen. The wise men who enacted the law could not have had even a faint perception of what in a pinch could be called a seaman. It would have been a rare bargain for the captain had he been able to trade the four ordinaries for one real sailor, even a very black one.

The ordinaries were certainly ordinary in a sense which in some parts of the United States is pronounced "ornery." Had they not been members of our crew they would have been inmates of a poorhouse or a jail. One of them had but one eye which, however, was all he needed as he had nothing to look for but the next meal. Two of them named Riley and Murphy had but one pair of pants between them. Murphy would have to go below before Riley could come on deck. How they got on board was a problem which had probably been solved by some boardinghouse keeper, and their method or means of getting on shore would also have to be solved by others, for the solving of problems was not in the line of their mental activities.

It was a twelve-day trip from Boston to Liverpool with fine weather and smooth water all the time. Her schedule under less favorable conditions would no doubt have been a few additional days. The cattle were tended by what were known as "stiffs," men who had ventured to the golden shores but when seized with the pangs of homesickness had dropped everything in a mad desire to be once more at home with mother. Homesickness is a terrible affliction. Those who are affected are blind to everything around them. The most heavenly beauties make no appeal. Opportunities which may be ready to jump down their throats are ignored; everything but the idea of an instant return to their old home is scorned by the homesick one. To set foot again in the place of his birth—even though it be the most wretched and unappealing spot on the globe—is all he asks of the world. Nearly everyone has had some opportunity to diagnose this feeling. Some of the natives of my East Anglian village would have felt the pangs of homesickness had they been taken as much as ten miles from their hearthstone. I knew a young man who went to America under the most favorable conditions. When he landed in New York, in compliance with a promise he had made his mother, he mailed a postcard. Then, glancing around at all the strange sights that met his view, he made immediately for a steamer just ready to depart and reached home ahead of his postcard. Once when I was mackerel fishing on the west coast of England, we put into Penzance, the first port we had entered. Among our crew was a fine-looking young man who had decided to take up fishing as a means of livelihood. It was his first trip. He was not seasick and appeared promising. When the boat's bow touched the pier at Penzance, he jumped on shore and ran, leaving his few effects and his money behind him. This was before hitchhiking became a popular means of travel and when stealing a ride—had such a thing been possible on an English train—would have meant a penitentiary sentence. Our deserter walked home and he stayed there.

These penniless wretches on this old boat who fed and watered cattle in return for the trip home would have embraced an opportunity to again reach dear old England had they, as part of the contract, been obliged to sleep with the cattle and share their food. At that, eliminating the risk of being trod on by a big steer, their sleeping quarters were no improvement on those occupied by the cattle, and their food was not much better than the dried corn on the cob which they fed their charges. This ship had a special brand of sea biscuits, the recipe for which may have been a company secret. They would not absorb water and if put to soak overnight they floated around in the morning as dry and buoyant as life preservers. We also had a special pack of salt beef, which had been in brine until it was quite black and when cut with a knife showed a surface of metallic appearance somewhat like layers of iron pyrites which appear in some kinds of coal. This beef had probably been preserved for years and may have been part of a reserve intended for use on Nelson's ships. It was what I believe is termed "commercial beef," the kind that can be stored in warehouses and bonds issued, using the beef as security. I discussed this experience just recently with the man in charge of the sub-basement in the British Museum—where the mummies are kept. He said it was not unusual, that he had served for some time in the British Navy and that on one occasion when they took on supplies for a cruise, all of the salt beef which came on board was branded "1812." It would be a hardy adventurer who made the second attempt for a fortune in America after going home as a "stiff" on a cattle boat. The ship was alive with rats which scampered over us when we slept or, for that matter, whenever we lay down. The crew seemed to regard them as a part of the condition of life. If there is any meaning in the statement that rats will leave a doomed ship, this old boat must have been a particularly good risk from the rats' viewpoint.

I had now tried steamboating and farming in America and concluded that neither of these lines had much to recommend them above deep-sea trawling. Soon I was back at my familiar tasks, hoping that someday I would see a route open before me to a more desirable existence.

There were many characters along the docks at Lowestoft who managed to eke out some sort of an existence without ever going beyond the outer piers, for once outside those piers life assumed an unwavering earnestness. Among these different waterfront types was a boy of thirteen or fourteen years of age who had the peculiar ability of being able to imitate the voice of the harbor master. The docks were owned by the Great Eastern Railway Company. The volume of business handled through this small port was enormous. Besides the herring and mackerel fishing boats, of which there were some hundreds, there was a large fleet, another three or four hundred of deep-sea trawlers. In addition to all the commerce created by the fishing fleets, quite a few warehouses were located on the water front, and many cargo steamers and ships discharged or loaded cargoes at Lowestoft. The railway company kept three large tugboats in readiness to bring ships into port or to facilitate their departure.

The official representative of the railway company, the harbor master, was a burly man with grey whiskers and a very red face, and a decided whiskey-and-soda appearance. He had three assistant harbor masters under him, all of whom trembled visibly when he spoke, if they were near enough to hear him, and that would be anywhere within a radius of a quarter of a mile. He caused the crews of the boats much unnecessary annoyance and trouble by arbitrarily changing their moorings. No sooner would they be berthed at one dock than he would order them to another. One of his deputies usually followed him carrying an axe. If mooring ropes were not promptly released, he would order them cut. Fortunately, he usually limited his overlording to the larger craft and sometimes would not be seen on the docks for a day or two, which fact might indicate that occasionally in a bout with the whiskey and soda he had come off second best.

The aforementioned boy, who slept in fish barrels and picked up his meals among the cooks on the boats, would sneak along behind the harbor master and give contra and confusing orders. So well did he imitate the bellow of the harbor master that his orders were usually obeyed. He was the bane of the harbor master's life but created much fun and diversion along the docks.

(169)

One day a very large ship came into port. She had been a long time on the voyage and had evidently passed through tropical climes. There were parrots and other highly colored birds in cages on the poop deck. Her sails, which were clewed up, were almost snow white. It was a great occasion for the harbor master. He personally took charge of getting her to her berth. The town of Lowestoft is divided by the river Waveney. The older and more important business section is on the north side. The leading hotel, most of the tourist attractions, and a great many of the residences are on the south side. One narrow bridge connects the two sections of the town—wholly inadequate fifty years ago but still unimproved. For ships passing into the inner harbor, it is necessary to open the bridge and hold up traffic until the ship had passed through. This was of frequent occurrence. Sometimes before the traffic could clear up another ship or boat would approach, and they had by all means the right of way. The channel where the bridge crossed was only about two feet or so wider than this ship. She had been brought in with the start of the flood tide, as this facilitated her movements.

For some purpose at one time, but no longer in use, water pipes had been run along the dock under the platform and when no longer in use had been disconnected but left there. A break in the pipe permitted one at the end of the dock to shout an order down the pipe which would appear to come from someone on the dock above and almost at the point where the bridge crossed.

The ship moved slowly with hausers from each quarter and also from both bows. It was a critical situation. The harbor master had ordered the bridge opened long before such action was necessary. Traffic backed up for half a mile on each side of the river. Flanked by two of his assistants, wearing his finest uniform very much trimmed with gold braid, his pilot jacket buttoned tightly over his expansive stomach, purple with excitement and the sense of his own importance, he shouted orders from the dock: "Vast heaving on the starboard bow line!" "Port your helm!" "Starboard your helm!" The crew of the ship were wild with suppressed excitement. An order was given and almost instantly canceled or nullified by the next one. The ship had an anchor hanging from each bow. Every precaution had been taken; it was a great event, for the town, for the railway company, and for the harbor master. If everything moved smoothly, other big ships might discharge their cargoes there. Just when the ship was opposite the bridge and commands were being shouted to do this and do that, the voice of the harbor master rang out: "Let go the anchor!" A frenzied sailor dropped one of the anchors. The order had come from the boy friend through the disused water pipe. The incoming tide carried the ship ahead over the anchor. It took two or three hours to recover the anchor. By that time every cart, and most of the population of the town were on one or the other side of the river waiting for the little bridge to turn so they could pass over. The boy was not seen on the docks for weeks; he evidently had gone inland. Perhaps he tried crow scaring and thistle digging, which would have been great aids in showing him the error of his ways.

I continued to be steadily employed on the trawlers. One day during winter when we had ventured down the Dutch coast to within sight of the Heligoland Island Light, I was sitting on deck splicing a rope. We were "hove to" with a strong wind which our skipper had said he was sure would soon moderate. He was one of those optimists who could see the sun shining in a blinding snowstorm. The north coast of Holland is one of the most treacherous in the world. In some places, when out of sight of the low islands off the coast, there would be but ten fathoms of water. With a strong wind, the sea would soon become very dangerous. Also the tide, strange to relate, runs to the eastward almost continuously, making it nearly impossible for any sailing craft to get out into deep water when a strong westerly or northwesterly gale was blowing. While we were out in twenty fathoms of water, the sea was rough out of all proportion to the force of the wind. Suddenly the boat gave an ominous lurch to windward.

I looked around to see a cliff of green water coming over the side. Water is nearly as heavy as sand. Hand hold means nothing in withstanding such a pressure. It is necessary to be to windward of something immovable and even then one may experience broken bones from the impact of the water. I could reach the trawl net which was fast to the trawl beam but had time for nothing more than that and, throwing myself flat on the deck face downward, I was swept against the cabin skylight, knocking the top off it with my head. The wave went across the full length of the trawler taking out almost all of the lee bulwarks carrying away the boat and, from the force of the impact, the hatches were blown out and carried away. For a short time we were in a sad plight, but sail was rapidly shortened and spare sails were nailed over the hatchways. I had a chance for a moment to consider myself. Blood was streaming down my face. I went below and, with the aid of a 4 x 6 mirror, saw that my nose was entirely flat with my face and a long gash ran along the top of my head. I pulled my nose out where it belonged and molded it into shape. Fortunately, I set it in such a manner as left it looking no worse than before the accident and also at an angle which has since kept it quite successfully out of other people's business. It was three days before we reached port. My eyes had swollen so nearly closed that I could not see the compass. I was helped on shore and taken to a doctor. After waiting all these years to meet a doctor professionally, this one promptly told me that nothing could be done on account of the swelling. It was six weeks before I was again ready for sea when I was given the berth which I had had to surrender on account of the injury.

One day when we came into port I learned that our vessel was going into drydock for painting. Other overhauling work was to be done to prepare her for the winter season. I would have a few days' lay-off, a circumstance which at first I welcomed. The next day, dressed in my best "shore clothes," I strolled along the dock. I stopped for a moment to watch some men getting supplies on board a small trawler which had her name on her stern in large gilt letters—*Bessie Pepper*. Directly I stopped, a man stepped forward and said to me: "Looking for a berth, my boy?" I told him I was not; that I had only come on shore the day previous. However, the man, who proved to be the fortunate owner of the *Bessie Pepper*, continued as though I had not spoken. He evidently did not consider the first "no" as an answer in the negative. He said: "We need a third hand for this vessel." Calling a forty-eight ton trawler a vessel was a bit flattering to the trawler, but she was his boat and he could call her whatever he wished. I stated that I had never been third hand. He then asked me how long I had been at sea and when I told him, "Four years," he at once decided that I would qualify as third hand. A third hand on a trawler with only five in the crew would stand a six-hour watch each night and often spend most of that time on deck alone. Besides having his own life and that of his shipmates in his hands, he could be a serious menace to other craft which crossed his course if he did not know how to handle the clumsy trawler and carefully observe the rules of the road. To support his offer, the owner said: "Let me call the skipper on shore and have him talk to you." The skipper came on shore, a tough-looking old fellow with close set beady eyes, a large purple-colored nose, and a generally murderous and forbidding appearance. He agreed with the owner that I was or would be a most competent third hand, this without asking any questions. So, slightly against my wishes and wholly in opposition to my judgment, I was made third hand of the *Bessie Pepper*, with the admonition that we would sail early in the morning, the owner qualifying the skipper's statement by repeating, "Very early."

The crew of a Lowestoft trawler, at any time during the past one hundred years, consisted of the skipper, mate—usually called out of Lowestoft the second hand—third hand, deck hand, and cook. The owner, who had now added my time to his payroll expense, wanted to get the boat out early. He had learned that no fish are caught while the boat is in port, while the overhead is about the same as when the boat is at sea. To further this idea and as an expression of his sense of personal reponsibility, he was on the dock himself the next morning when I arrived before daylight. A strong and bitterly cold wind was blowing from the east. The sea was breaking over the south pier. The whole prospect was most discouraging. But the owner displayed an enthusiasm which was intended to be more than an offset. The skipper was quite drunk, a hangover from a party of the previous evening which had been extended almost to the hour of our proposed sailing. We got the boat out to the inner pier and then discovered that we had no cook. In numbers, if not in efficiency, this left us short twenty per cent of our crew. The owner dashed off up town to look for a cook in the dark but he returned without one. He asked the skipper if in the meantime he had found a cook. The skipper had found a near-by pub and was re-enlivening his fading state of inebriation. He answered the owner's questions as though he did not know what it was all about. Returning from his third trip—it was now light enough to see stray cooks if any were running around—the owner brought a cook with him. That trawler had to be gotten to sea at all costs. The skipper returned from a final trip to the pub. We had already hoisted the mainsail and mizzen which were flapping in the wind.

The cook, who had detoured around by his home,

arrived carrying his belongings in a pillow slip. He was accompanied not only by the owner but also by a man who worked for the railway company on the docks. Approaching me, this man inquired, "Are you one of the crew of the *Bessie Pepper?*" I rather reluctantly admitted that I was, although I was beginning to wish it had been otherwise. "Well," he said, "this boy, Abraham, has been lodging with me." His interest in the "boy" or the reason for it was at once apparent. The "boy" was no doubt in arrears for his lodging. He added: "He has never been to sea, and I want you to take care of him." Abraham was at least my own age, a tall and apparently very much underfed young man. I had a full realization of the responsibility I had assumed by accepting the berth of third hand. To add to that the duties of the cook appeared to be placing further responsibility where it was not needed, but there was no escape: I agreed to "take care" of Abraham and was afterwards glad that I had done so, when I learned that he had for a long time been an orphan. He had no "career" behind him, and it would not have needed the opinion of a "seer" to draw the conclusion that he had none immediately before him. He was bundled on board and the now thoroughly drunken skipper with him.

One of the railway company's big tugboats with two funnels and power enough to have towed a battleship took our tow rope. The owner cast off the mooring ropes and no doubt cast off a lot of worry at the same time. The *Bessie Pepper* was going to sea and almost on time. There could be no doubt but that she was going somewhere with that powerful tug fast to her. The waves were breaking on the bar at the entrance to the harbor, but this did not deter the tugboat, which went buoyantly over them, but the waves were steep. The *Bessie Pepper,* with her low freeboard had no chance to mount them so she went under them. The decks were filled with water, but soon we were over the bar and in better water. Abraham had retired to the cabin. The tugboat gave us a safe offing and cast off. We got in the tow rope, hoisted the stay foresail with the sheet to windward and ran out the jib. The skipper went below; he was helplessly drunk. The mate took the tiller and gave the order to "let draw." The foresail was trimmed to leeward, and the *Bessie Pepper,* under a single reef in the mainsail and a six-cloth jib, was on her way.

Abraham's nautical career had commenced. In an attempt to make a forty-eight-ton boat do the work of one of sixty tons, the *Bessie Pepper* had been very much oversparred and then to counteract that error, she was heavily ballasted to give her rigidity to carry her masts. She was almost as lacking in buoyancy as a water-soaked log. I went below and read the Lowestoft *Journal,* a copy of which I had brought on board with the current number of *Ally*

Sloper. Abraham was soon in that physical and mental condition where a man is willing to give a shilling, if he has one, to be thrown overboard. The skipper was merely soused. When we had passed outside the sandbars which parallel that part of the English coast, the mate gave the helm to the deck hand and he also came below. The deck hand did not appear to be an expert helmsman, and the *Bessie Pepper* was wholly lacking in any spirit of co-opera-tion. She would not raise her bows to the waves but plunged through them, shipping great quantities of water. The spray was dashed up into the weather part of the mainsail, causing it to shrink and leaving the leech slack. As we were close hauled, this allowed the leech of the sail to flicker, causing a considerable vibration in the hull. The *Bessie Pepper* had been in port for a few days. The drainage from her last catch of fish was still in the bilge. The motion of the boat stirred the bilge water and created a ter-rible stench. The panels in the cabin, the copper coins in our pockets, and probably our lungs, had we been able to see them, turned the color of pewter from the foul odor.

I cooked dinner without asking Abraham to watch how it was done; boiled salt beef, a suet pud-ding, and potatoes boiled in their skins. The skipper had sobered up enough to eat his dinner and took the helm while the deck hand ate his. He continued to steer part of the afternoon while the mate, the deck hand, and I got things in order for the work which would commence when we reached the fishing ground. With the exception of Abraham, we were accustomed to the conditions. We ate our dinners in the foul-smelling cabin; we overhauled the trawl and did other necessary things which were a part of what was always required. Abraham had no interest in dinner, his misery was complete. Neither the smell of the bilge water, the vibration caused by the slack in the sail, nor the constant pitching of the boat could add anything to Abraham's feeling of utter despair.

We sailed all day and all of the night and the next day to reach the spot where the skipper had decided that the fish were waiting for us. The first night I steered for six hours without relief or interruption, the *Bessie Pepper* continuing to plunge joyously through the waves. Soon I had opportunity for more intimate acquaintance with my shipmates. We arrived on the fishing grounds, the weather moderated, Abraham returned to life but did not for some time show much action. The trawl was put down, and the next morning we had fried fish for breakfast. By this time Abraham was feeling much better and manifested an interest in the frying fish. I gave him his first lesson in how to fry fish. I explained: "Always have plenty of fat in the pan, have the pan very hot before you put the fish in and keep it hot. Fish won't cook in lukewarm fat.

"The *Bessie Pepper* continued to plunge joyously through the waves."

Do not put wet fish in the pan as they make the fat sputter. Don't turn the fish till they are white on the upper side. Lots of heat and plenty of fat are the requisites for frying fish." Soon Abraham was able to fry the fish. Cooking dinner was more simple. Not much skill is required to boil salt beef or potatoes with their skins on. Making suet pudding was not a very complicated matter. I showed Abraham how to chop the suet, as the "suet" often was not suet and even when it was, after being in the brine for awhile, it was quite refractory as to chopping fine. Even sprinkling flour on it would not always save the day or the situation. Experience gave me a slight advantage in dealing with the suet. When Abraham was left to his own resources he did the best he could. He got the suet into the pudding but often in unreasonably large chunks which the mate, if he were fortunate enough to draw one in his helping of pudding, would call "horses' eyes." On Sunday we had plum pudding which was just the same as the pudding we had on Saturday plus a few raisins.

Drunk or sober, the skipper was never bashful in telling about his past life, the high spots of which had been numerous love affairs. I thought he would have been the perfect mate for my childhood neighbor, Mrs. Snobey, but it was too late to now consider that possibility. The mate was a fat, good-natured fellow who had but little to say on any subject. The deck hand was a real character. He styled himself "Jumbo"; he was short in stature and hardly made up for it in width. Abraham had only just commenced to make history and had none of it to relate.

I was interested in Jumbo and asked him what his real name was, but he said he had no name other than Jumbo. He had been raised in some institution. If he had ever had parents, he did not know their name or who they were. He had been given a name in the "home," which he did not like, and when he left that place he left his name behind him. He had already served a five-year apprenticeship to the desirable calling of deep-sea trawler but so far had not been able to select a name to his liking and continued as merely Jumbo. He was now earning fourteen shillings a week and his board. So far the world had not dealt very kindly with Jumbo. He did not appear to harbor very fond memories of the "home." The man to whom he had given five years of his life in order to qualify as deck hand of the *Bessie Pepper* had been a harsh taskmaster. He owned several trawlers, which he manned as far as possible with apprentices who drew no pay and only had food and clothing for their labors. The law pertaining to apprentices was very definite. If the apprentice was thirteen at the time he signed the articles, he could be held to the completion of his period of service. If he ran away, he was subject to arrest and imprisonment, after which he was returned to his owner very much as a runaway slave would be. Jumbo stated that, on account of his master having so many apprentices, he bought their clothing in dozen lots and all of the same size. Jumbo had spent the five years in man-size clothing, but it had not helped his physical expansion. The only clothes provided were blue woollen shirts, guernseys, and duffle trousers. Clothing with exposed buttons could not be worn. The buttons might become caught in the heavy net and the wearer dragged overboard with the trawl. Jumbo's employer or temporary owner had been in the habit of transferring apprentices from a trawler arriving in port to one which was ready to leave. This gave the boys the maximum of opportunity to learn the profession they had selected but deprived them of all opportunity for change or recreation. In the "home" Jumbo had been taught to read. He was fascinated with the stories of large fortunes or estates which were held in chancery awaiting the claims of their rightful owners. Sometimes—but probably rarely—the fortunate heirs would come into their own or any such part of it as the lawyers did not need. Advertisements appeared in the papers offering the aid of "experts" in making these recoveries. No one else could possibly have been more interested in this subject than was Jumbo. To him, it held a double claim for interest; he first had to find out who he was then later trace the records for his claims to fortunes and estates then held in chancery. The people at the "home" had been quite uncommunicative as to his antecedents and quite likely did not have any knowledge themselves of who his parents were or how he had happened to become one of their flock. The largest sum of money he had ever possessed at one time before his apprenticeship was finished was threepence. However, he was a free man at last and able to earn fourteen shillings a week, a part of which could be used to develop his meagre wardrobe. He was cheerful under the harsh condition of his life, but at this time there was a vast amount of wisdom which he had not absorbed.

The skipper was fond of telling of his exploits and revealing the intimacies of his past life. The wisdom derived from that extensive experience he seemed most anxious to communicate to me. The mate was neither an understanding nor an appreciative listener. The skipper could not be on terms of equality, much less of intimacy, with Jumbo and Abraham on account of their rank in the trawler's crew. As Abraham's life held no thrills for his own reflective pleasure or for a listener if he had one, as the mate did not wish to talk, and as when Jumbo had finished his brief history he had no more to relate, the skipper furnished most of the conversation. Except for his exaggerated egotism and his use of the most awful profanity, the skipper was not a bad old fellow, but Abraham was at all times in mortal terror of him. His murderous appearance and terrible language were a combination to which Abraham's nerves were not equal. The skipper confided in me that, while his wife had stood loyally by him, his children had been a great disappointment. The girls had never been of any help to him, and the boys had robbed him.

One day when we were detained in port, much to our owner's distress, the skipper as usual when given time to do so got gloriously drunk and in that condition came on board. Just as he stepped on deck a man carrying some much enlarged and very handsomely retouched photographs also came on board. No one was interested in the artist or his samples until he accosted the skipper. The skipper was not interested, but he was too drunk to say so. The artist sensed a prospect. The skipper's resistance was weakened by his alcoholic content, and he was defenseless against the salesman's line of argument. He was easily persuaded to have his picture taken as a present for his wife. The "samples" were freely displayed: pictures of men still living—though they might not have recognized themselves—and only waiting for them to return to port and accept delivery. After smashing the skipper's very feeble resistance, the artist's troubles were not ended. There was difficulty in getting a pose owing to the fact that the skipper could not stand erect. He was finally supported in the rigging and the camera snapped. Only one picture was taken, the artist no doubt fearing that a second would be worse than the first. Half the cost of the finished picture was paid and in so far as the skipper was concerned, it was forgotten. But, when we next arrived in port, no sooner had the bow of the *Bessie Pepper* touched the dock than our artist friend stepped on board carrying a picture of the skipper, which to say the least was very much "overdone." Having been at sea three weeks, the skipper was as sober as any man living. The artist explained the verbal agreement, called attention to his work; even the nose had about the proper purple tint, but no retouching could disguise the fact that it was a picture of a very drunken man. To salvage what he had already invested in the venture, the skipper paid the balance, took the picture home to his wife, whose loyalty still ran high enough to permit her to praise its "naturalness."

We continued our cruises. Our diet had never varied from the fried fish for breakfast, salt beef, suet pudding, and potatoes for dinner, leftovers or just sea biscuits for supper. The skipper one day remarked to Abraham: "I want a baking powder pudding for dinner tomorrow."

"Yes, yes," the cook replied, but he was much disturbed. Just when he thought he had mastered all the intricacies of cooking, here was a new demand made on him. He had long before become independent of my guidance in the preparation of the meals. Now he would have to take more "lessons." He referred his new problem to me.

"How do you make a baking powder pudding?" he asked.

I told him: "I will have to show you; that will be easier than telling you."

The next forenoon Abraham routed me out of a much needed sleep to show him how to make baking powder pudding. I told him to put fresh water in the boiler for baking powder pudding could not be cooked in salt water. Then, mixing flour, water, and baking powder, I tied the pudding in a cloth which had been made by ripping open a flour sack. I fastened it loosely, which brought comment from my pupil, but I explained that this was different from a suet pudding in that it must have room to expand. I had taught him to tie suet pudding very tightly or, when cooked in salt water, the pudding would become impregnated with the salt water. We did not carry enough fresh water to permit of its general use in cooking. I told Abraham to cook the pudding for forty-five minutes. It proved to be no worse when served with treacle—as the black molasses was called—than the suet pudding which we had been eating previously. However, the skipper and mate each took extra helpings, which left none for the other two members of the crew. This slight was too much for Jumbo. He did not know all the rights and privileges of a British subject but he knew he should have pudding and he roundly cursed the cook—the greatest humiliation to which Abraham had so far been subjected—for not making the pudding larger.

The next day I was on deck and, happening to glance down the cabin skylight, I saw the cook busily preparing dinner. He had apparently put all the flour on board in the two dishpans which were used both in the preparation and the serving of the food. Dinner was late, but presently Abraham appeared on deck wearing a most lugubrious expression. He never washed except when he was going on shore, even had we stayed at sea for a month. His begrimed face was streaked with perspiration. "I wish you'd come below," he said. I went down the cabin. The large convex boiler—we had but three utensils in which to cook anything: the frying pan, the boiler, and the teakettle—was on the stove, the lid some two inches from the top.

"Take it off the fire," I told him. The boiler was placed on the cabin floor, and Abraham tried to pull the pudding out, but it had expanded into the convex sides of the boiler and could not be withdrawn. It was removed in sections and was found to be cooked, for about two inches, on the outside; the center was still dough. Everybody had all the pudding they could eat. The skipper in utter disgust shouted at Abraham: "God sends food, but the devil sends such cooks as you." We had slices of the pudding fried with the fish for breakfast. We ate it every night for supper until it finally soured and had to be thrown overboard. There were no more changes in our diet for some time.

It was now midwinter and bitterly cold much of the time. The usual winter gales swept across the North Sea, and nothing in their course was much less adequate to resist them than the poor little *Bessie Pepper* with her motley little crew. All hands were kept on deck almost continuously, and much of the time we were wet to the skin. The *Bessie Pepper* needed close watching because of her generally poor seaworthiness. When the trawl was down it was necessary to keep all the sail on her which she could carry, because her trawl was much too heavy for a boat of her tonnage. The skipper was far from being the man he had once been if any measure of credence was given his many stories. Drink and a hard life were already taking their toll in lowered resistance and the inability to supply the leadership needed. The mate, like myself, had been raised on plain food and had a fine physique though a none too active mentality. Both Jumbo and Abraham were poorly supplied with clothing. To Jumbo, this did not matter so much. Lack of sleep, cold and privation had always been his lot, but Abraham was not, and could not, be developed into the type suited for such an arduous life. The fact that he was orphaned at an early age might indicate low physical resistance on the part of his parents.

One day some weeks later when we were in port, the skipper ordered a small package of dried peas brought on board. These Abraham carefully concealed. He did not know anything about dried peas and wished to avoid further culinary experiments. Temporarily they were forgotten, but when the skipper did recall the purchase, he gave peremptory orders for peas for dinner on the following day. I was called upon for a recipe for cooking dried peas. I said: "Soak them in fresh water overnight, tie them in a cloth, and cook them in fresh water for two hours." "That's all?" "Yes, that is all." The next day I was on deck when the cook was preparing to serve dinner. I heard the peas as he poured them from the cloth into one of the dishpans. They rattled like shot; cooking them had made them tougher than before that experience. Raw, they were somewhat brittle; cooked, they were as tough as lead. Abraham was cursed for ever having been born. Later, he turned on his instructor, remarking: "I cooked those peas just as you told me to and see what happened." I had to acknowledge that the fault was mine; I had not cooked peas for a long time.

"I should have told you to put some soda in with

the peas, or a piece of coal." Any cook knows the potent qualities of soda. I have never studied chemistry and do not know the different elements in coal. Anyway, while we had more coal than soda on board, Abraham used soda the next time which was the day following. The peas were cooked all right this time. They could have been eaten through a soda fountain straw, they were so completely dissolved. However, they were very bitter, a fact which neither the skipper nor the mate seemed to notice. As I held back, and as Jumbo and the cook were again forgotten, the two senior members of the crew ate the whole batch, and Abraham received another profane rebuke from Jumbo. It was the custom for the three senior members of the crew to eat their dinner first; the deck hand and cook would have whatever was left, if anything were left, but in the case of the peas, as also the first baking powder pudding, there was nothing left for the second table or rather the second service from the cabin floor. These social or class distinctions may be the best rule of life. Not many people seem quite happy unless they have some "inferiors" around them; neither do they seem quite satisfied unless there is someone higher up who can produce in them the proper feeling of respect and humility. To eat at the second service—when anything was left to eat—may have been best for Jumbo and Abraham, good for their souls perhaps. In the case of these peas, it was certainly well for their physical bodies. Shortly after dinner the skipper and mate were both seized with sharp abdominal pains. The mate went below; the better place to him appeared to be his bunk. But the skipper stayed on deck; his curses changed to groans, and finally he ended up in the lee scuppers, his clothing in disarray, a grey ghostly pallor on his face; even his nose was somewhat faded. Both the boys were badly scared, and I was not enjoying the situation. I had never known a trawler to die from the effects of anything he had eaten. As I had eaten of everything that my superiors had had except the peas, I readily concluded that the peas must be the cause of the trouble. The wind freshened, sail had to be shortened, a demand which in the case of the *Bessie Pepper* was imperative; no trifling with her on that score. Her long masts and oversize sails did not permit it. With the help of my two young shipmates, the mainsail was reefed but it then appeared necessary to take a reef in the mizzen and shift jibs. Reefing the mizzen was a small matter, and shifting jibs would have taken but a few minutes had not Abraham, with a nervous desire to be helpful—a desire which possibly had its roots in a sense of guilt on his part and a feeling of impending disaster for which he would have to answer—released the jib halyards before the sail was brought in. He discovered his mistake and belayed the halyards but not until enough slack had been given the weather rope to permit the wind to get behind the sail, causing it to flap and whip the chain halyards around the lee arm of the crosstrees. We now had a difficult situation to deal with. Jumbo, who had more courage than the elephant he was named for, crawled head first out on the lee crosstree, trying to get the jib halyard clear. It was getting dark, the boat was tossing and pitching, the halyards were a heavy chain. It took us a long time to get that jib in and a smaller one set in its place. When this was finally done, I turned my attention to the poor old skipper who was lying as though dead. I dragged him to the companionway; the boys both went below to help get him down the cabin. The boat gave a lurch at the wrong moment; they did not have a secure grip on the skipper, and he went down to the cabin floor in a heap. He was picked up and laid on the lee locker where he stayed till the next day.

Abraham handed me up the side lights but neither he nor the deck hand returned on deck. I stayed on deck till four in the morning when I went below to get the mate to come on deck and relieve me, or at least to learn how he was feeling. To my surprise he was not in his berth. A sliding door opened from the cabin to the hold. Pushing this back and striking a match and looking in the hold, I found the mate lying on the iced fish. I got him into the cabin, but he protested when I proposed that he come on deck and relieve me. He said he was sick and unable to climb the ladder. However, I gave him lots of help and soon had him on deck. We were hove to, had been hove to all night, as I had not felt that I had quite enough man power in the persons of Jumbo and Abraham to put down the trawl. We had lost a whole night's fishing on account of the overcooked, or chemically treated, peas. This would have been bad news for our owner had it ever reached his ears.

When I turned out in the morning, Jumbo was in charge of the deck. The skipper was still lying where he had been stretched out the evening before but as he was breathing I felt there was no further cause for alarm. Later in the day he was able to sit up with his back supported by the bulkhead. He did not eat any breakfast but made a feeble attempt at eating dinner. Abraham's face wore an appearance of cheerfulness which was most certainly assumed. Both the skipper and the mate recovered, the mate being first to regain normality because of his youth and greater vigor. Even when the skipper was again fully restored, neither he nor the mate made any mention of the peas. They had been hogs to eat so many, and a sense of guilt on that score may have kept them silent. The skipper must privately have sworn off on any further faddist food, for as long as I stayed with the *Bessie Pepper* there was never any variation from the regular bill. Later Abraham confided in me that he had put a piece of soda as large as his fist in the cloth with the peas. But after that time he never had to cook anything but the fried fish, salt beef, suet pudding, and potatoes. The use of potatoes was always restricted, for they were considered as a sort of luxury.

While our time was divided into watches—the mate and third hand splitting the night into two six-hour watches and taking the afternoon watch on alternate days—we were sometimes on deck so long that we could not remember who really had the last watch or was due to take the next. The ordinary work incidental to handling the sails on such a large boat was often sufficient to keep the crew busily engaged. Added to this was the lowering and raising of the trawl, gutting fish, packing them in ice, mending the net—never-ending tasks. I had plenty of opportunity while on the trawlers, and particularly while on the *Bessie Pepper,* to observe the effect of water on the skin. Nothing but a fish can stand as much soaking as a human being. When the water was smooth, the decks of the *Bessie Pepper* amidships were but slightly above the water level. When at all rough, she carried water almost constantly in her lee scuppers. There was no place to dry clothes except on one's back. We were wet through almost continuously; we did not bother to change and had we done so we should have soon been out of "changes." We usually turned in "all standing," meaning with all our clothes on ready to answer a hasty summons on deck. When a squall struck the *Bessie Pepper*, it was only a matter of self-preservation to get on deck instantly and stand by to shorten sail. It was said if one "turned in wet," they would "wake up steaming," which we did without any apparent ill effect. Quite robust health was necessary to enable any man to long endure the exposure to which the crews of the trawlers were constantly subjected.

After awhile I left the *Bessie Pepper* and my friends, Jumbo and Abraham, who continued with her. The skipper almost wept at parting with me—I had been such a good listener to his stories. On one of my trips to England in later years, when I visited Lowestoft as I have always done, I saw Jumbo and learned of Abraham's sad fate. Abraham was not lacking in spirit or courage. He had forced himself to endure the hardships of the trawler's life for awhile but he developed tuberculosis and was put on shore where he lay down and died.

I sailed on other and finer boats than the *Bessie Pepper*, but poor ships make good sailors. At one time I was third hand on one of the trawlers which had been built by the Baroness Burdett-Coutts. This great philanthropist had, like Doctor Grenfell, heard of the sufferings and hardships that the North Sea trawlers were subjected to. She was anxious to help, but the only way to help anyone is by the Grenfell route: teach them to help themselves. To do this one must sit at their table—if they have a table —or eat with them from the cabin floor and share their lives in every way. This the good Baroness could not do. But she spent a lot of money trying to improve their lot. It did not help any more than the credit which Smith and Lark extended to the villagers in the parish where I was born.

At age twenty-two, I was mate of a fine sixty-four-ton trawler named the *Julia May*, the skipper of which, aged twenty-eight, was the oldest man on board. I was then receiving about one eighth of the trawler's earnings as my compensation, the skipper an amount fractionally larger, and the rest of the money going to the owner, who provided the boat and paid the other three members of the crew their weekly wages. I was steadily employed and put my surplus earnings—as I was at sea almost all the time, my earnings, except what was needed for clothes, were mostly surplus—in the savings bank, and got as much pleasure out of life as was possible under such conditions. But I felt that somewhere, under other conditions, a more agreeable life must be attainable.

During the past few years I had done a good deal of—and for the most part quite unprofitable—reading. During the summer months when we would sometimes be becalmed, I had plenty of time for reading. I bought books from second-hand bookstores but instead of considering the merits of the authors, I thought only of how much I was getting for my money. In volume I got some rare bargains. One dealer sold me a number of bound volumes of the *Sunday at Home,* all I could carry for a shilling. They were of dates some twenty to thirty years previous and were illustrated with wood cuts. These large volumes—no other member of the crew ever looked at them—gave the impression that I must be an unusually well-informed person. I bought a dictionary to help me with the harder words. I was a teetotaler, because I did not and have never liked the taste of either liquor or beer. A man who did not drink beer and who read books —and such large ones—would necessarily be regarded as a freak. If anyone tried to make fun of my peculiarities, I could silence them with one remark. I would say: "I'll show you how to gut fish." This was always a vulnerable spot with anyone who claimed to be a trawler. However, there were "freaks" a-plenty on the trawlers as elsewhere. We had a "freak" for cook when I was at the "duffer's" fleet. He confided in me that he was staying at the fleet till the police quit looking for him, that he would leave one trawler when she came in and join another just ready to leave, never going off the dock. This man was thirty years of age; and he had a good education. He had been a sailor at some time previous. He was the only man in my ten years' experience at sea whom I saw cleaning his teeth. This he did by using a piece of the leg of a stocking which he would wet, then dip in the coal ashes under the stove. Cinders no doubt have some good scouring qualities, maybe better than dogfish skins.

The mate of one trawler with whom I sailed had an accordion. Accordions and concertinas were often found on boats. This mate was a freak because he played freak tunes. One night when we had just reduced the mainsail to a double reef and I had gone below, leaving the skipper and third hand on deck, the mate asked me: "How about a little music?" I told him I was sure the neighbors would not complain. He brought out his accordion and played the "Marseillaise" while the quivering hull of the old trawler pounded into the waves.

As I advanced in rank, my responsibilities increased. My hours for sleep were shorter. To observe the traditions of the calling, I must be able to ignore cold, hunger, and lack of sleep. I was gifted with a fine constitution and the fullest measure of health, but I was not insensible to cold and like Captain Rabbit I still needed some sleep. I had now spent over nine years of my life on the fishing smacks. If I continued and saved my money as I was then doing, I might someday own a trawler, but that would take several years, and I would still have to go to sea. However, I was earning so much more than it would have been possible for me to earn at anything on shore, that I had no choice but to continue at sea. One day when we were in port for a day or possibly part of a day—as it would have been hard to explain to our owner why we needed to be in port a whole day—I was walking up High Street, Lowestoft, when glancing in the window of a bookstore I noticed a large book with a red cover bearing the title in gilt letters, *A Thousand Ways To Make a Living.* This at once commanded my full attention. Here were nine hundred and ninety-nine ways of making a living other than by deep-sea trawling. Although I never entered shops such as this which sold new books, I went in and priced the volume. The figure was staggering, though I do not now recall the amount. It was certainly more than I would have had to pay for bound volumes of the *Sunday at Home* ever since that magazine had been in print. I finally convinced myself that, with nine hundred and ninety-nine more roads opened to me as routes to fortune, the book might be worth the exorbitant price which was asked. I could not take much time to consider the matter. The dealer had but one volume—had I not come along he might have it yet. Someone could step in any moment and snatch it from my grasp. I paid the price and tingling with excitement I walked back down the street with my purchase. Had I told any of my acquaintances how much I had paid for that book, I should in their estimation have passed at once out of the "freak" class into that of "just plain fools."

There was not much time for reading. It was October, and calms were infrequent. However, I deprived myself of enough sleep to glance through the magic pages. I quickly discovered that the book and I had both been sold at the same time. Who ever seriously thought that there are a thousand ways to make a living? Of course there are not, not even including the "crooked ways," of which I will admit there are many. However, there were more than three hundred occupations, trades, professions, and means of making a livelihood which it was safe to catalogue and print, but actually deep-sea trawling was not listed. The author or compiler no doubt had concluded that a deep-sea trawler could not read—and hence would not be a potential purchaser of the book—or he would not be a deep-sea trawler. He would learn something better. The book was a tragic disappointment. I had spent all that money for naught. Here I had before me a list of all the possibilities and opportunities which life had to offer from kitchen maid to admiral, all in clear type between red covers with a gilded title. There was not one line of effort in the three hundred and odd which were considered more or less briefly, mostly less briefly, for which I could qualify. If I aspired to be a butler, I must commence my training as a page. What chance had I at twenty-two of being accepted as a page in a lady's boudoir? All the trades required that one serve an apprenticeship; all the professions required a great deal more education than I was capable of absorbing even had I both the will and opportunity to do so. The occupations were mostly a lot of miscellaneous efforts for which a training equal to an apprenticeship would be necessary.

There were, however, two chapters which at least interested me. These two chapters dealt with emigration, without defining it either as an occupation, trade, or profession. Perhaps that was decided after the emigrant arrived in the new land or, at the earliest, not until he had purchased his ticket. I have thought since that possibly those who were interested in having people emigrate were back of the publication. The requirements of the trades, professions, and occupations were quite definite. The requirements of an emigrant, though not mentioned outright, appeared to be that he possess the price of the ticket. The first of these chapters dealt with the great opportunities for a Britisher in South Africa. Lions and tigers had always been, in my mind, associated with Africa. But they were not mentioned. They had, I concluded, been dealt with less kindly than the English crows. They had been shot to death or scared into regions still unexplored. I would not worry further about them. But the picture of South Africa had a lot of flaws in its composition. The principal inducement offered was low-priced land. The main crop mentioned was oats. With oat crops there might be crows; there certainly would be horses, and there would be thistles. I had dug my share of thistles, and horses, I thought, did not like me. I went on to the next chapter, which dealt with the Province of British Columbia. The rest of Canada was ignored, and well it might be. Salesmanship is a gift, and the writer of the article on British Columbia possessed that gift in wonderful measure. He could sell the Province or the emigrant, or whatever and whoever is concerned in such a transaction. The salesman for South Africa was a dud. He was trying to limit his sales to Britishers. Not so with the expansive chap who had started out to sell, or to populate, western Canada. Everybody was welcome: white, yellow, brown, or black. No color, race, or creed was being barred from that man-hungry land at that time. A long list of the Province's many great resources was given. If you wished to dispute it, you would have to go there for your proof, or to discover that the proof was lacking. And to get there, you would have to buy a ticket, which circumstance or the creation of it was the writer's main interest. Nothing that could be said in Eng-

lish was left unsaid, and when no more could be
written in prose, the writer or salesman plunged
into verse, the concluding lines of which were:

"In that fair region far away,
Shall labor find employment,
A fair day's work, a fair day's pay,
And rest shall bring enjoyment."

British Columbia was a long way off. I knew that
much, but the writer had mentioned fish in abun-
dance. I had been raised on fish. If they could be
supplemented with a few turnips, I would be amply
provided for, and if the worst came to the worst,
there might be a chance to show my skill with the
fish, which were so plentiful. I committed the verse
to memory and weakened every time I ran it
through my mind. Soon I had decided that British
Columbia was the place for me. How strange! Today British Columbia has a population of less than
two persons to the square mile; England has seven
hundred to the square mile. That gushing writer
of nearly fifty years ago could no more describe
British Columbia than I can. I have made many
happy visits to this, indisputably, the loveliest province in the British Empire, but does such a statement
interest the average Britisher? It does not.

The next time I saw my parents I told them of
my decision. They were horrified. My father said:
"If you go all that way from home, we shall never

see you again." Under the stress of the situation, my father recalled that thirty years before two of his cousins had gone to America. He had never mentioned them and had probably forgotten they existed, but so far away a cousin would seem like a near relative. He would write some of his relatives and inquire if anyone had ever heard of the cousins since they left home. I returned to sea. Some time later my father supplied me with the address of both the cousins, one of whom actually bore our name— John Youell; his sister, Mrs. William Fisher, was the other cousin. They were both living in Grand Rapids, Michigan. This did not have much relation to British Columbia, but I could stop off there and later continue my journey to the "Land of Promise." I decided to write to Mrs. Fisher. I was twenty-two years old and had learned that men are often very practical, and my male half-cousin might not see how I could readily fit into a community where a large part of the workers were Dutch and proud of it. The principal industry was furniture making, and certainly the manufacturers could not readily find anyone who knew less about furniture than I did. Mrs. Fisher was not technical. She wrote me promptly and after stating that she did not know she had a cousin Tom—my father—she went on in answer to my request for advice saying that she thought anyone who was willing to work was better off in America than in England and should I decide to come to Michigan, she would be very pleased to welcome me. The world was, and still is, full of kind-hearted people who are anxious to help others.

It was now the month of March, almost six months after I had purchased the wonderful book. It had not been what could be termed a direct help, but it had been, by the narrow margin of one chapter, a guiding influence. It eventually led me from dear old England to the "Land of Opportunity." The winter of 1890 was a terribly cold one; no one could remember when it had been so cold. Gales of wind swept the North Sea almost continuously. But the *Julia May* was supposed to be more than a match for the elements. We entered port and departed again like a mail ship which had a schedule to maintain. When our catch of fish was discharged, our owner did not look at the sky to see what weather was promised or threatened. He looked at the mooring rope on the bollard which his fingers itched to be casting off. The *Julia May* was well found. Never could we make the excuse that anything was needed. Provisions, coal, or whatever was required had come on board before we had the fish on shore. If any repairs were needed to the rigging, that work was done by others. No need to wash down the decks after the fish was unloaded. The decks would be well washed before we had been long at sea. The owner attended to everything or had someone else do it, but always when we passed through the outer piers there were only five of us on board. Neither the owner nor his helpers cared to go outside the piers.

I finished my trawling experience on April 13, 1891. I should have finished one day earlier but a gale from the northwest was too much for even the *Julia May*. We had to "heave to" until it moderated. I gave my sea boots and oilskins to my shipmates, my dictionary to Dan Goodwin, the deck hand. Dan was quite well educated. He had educated himself, so he should have been satisfied with the job, but his education did not help in many of the tasks he was called upon to perform. The action of the tides was a problem which Dan could not work out. My dictionary had become almost unreadable from grease and dirt marks. I think it was sentiment on Dan's part that prompted him to ask me for it. When I told the owner I was leaving and going to America, he exhausted a vocabulary which was an acquisition of fifty years on the water front in trying to show me how many different kinds of a fool I was. However, neither his abuse nor his promise to make me a skipper of one of his trawlers as soon as I got a master's certificate had any effect on my purpose. The last three weeks I was at sea I had earned twenty-one pounds, which amount was considered a good earning at that time. Not many "trades, professions or occupations," would yield that amount. I was determined, however, to try

Michigan and, if that proved unsatisfactory, to go on to that "Fair region far away."

I went home to see my parents, packed my be-belongings in two tin trunks which were colored to look like wood, procured my ticket which was nearly as long as I was and which provided with a lot of other transportation a steerage passage on the steamer *Alaska,* which in the advertisements was described as the "Greyhound of the Atlantic." The "lurcher" of the Atlantic would have been equally appropriate. On the day before I was due to leave, a former schoolmate, George Elliott, looked me up. "I hear you are going to America, George." I told him I was leaving at eight in the morning. "Can I go with you?" I told him he could not get ready and get a ticket in time. He was sure he could get the ticket, and as he had nothing to get ready that was his only problem. He had a friend who had been converted to Mormonism and had gone to Utah, of which country the friend wrote almost as enthusiastically as had it been British Columbia. George was a man of action, and he started immediately for town, four miles away, on foot. He did not consider hiring a donkey. He had been places before but never more than ten miles from the spot where he was born, and he knew that the most reliable transportation in East Anglia was his legs.

At eight the next morning he met me at the station with a ticket longer than my own. Not many people could pack and prepare for a transoceanic journey in such a few hours. He had never needed but two shirts, to be worn on alternate weeks; he had his savings in the post office savings bank and not in a lot of clothes which might go out of style. He had been afraid to venture out to Utah alone but now that he had company he was ready to leave. George had, like the rest of us, been "compelled" to go to school until he had passed the fourth standard but he had not been compelled to study the geography of the United States, and I think had but a hazy idea as to where the stronghold of Mormonism was located. It took the entire day and transfers to three or four different railroads to go from Norwich to Liverpool. Our tickets provided for the night's lodging and for breakfast at Liverpool. We lacked nothing but the tags which are usually affixed to a box of rabbits or other live pets when they are being "sent by rail." When we arrived in Liverpool we were taken in charge by a guardian angel who no doubt represented the different equity holders in our four-foot tickets. We were quartered in a large building and for dinner we were each given a mutton chop, in some cases perhaps the first, and in more cases the last, time the emigrant would eat a chop from an English mutton. There must have been some subtle reason back of this mutton chop send-off. Possibly they wanted to impress us with the good things in store and avoid complications until we were safely on board the ship. Our sleeping quarters were a large room or dormitory over the mutton chop service dining room. The room contained two or three hundred cots. If any of the travelers had brought with them a contagious disorder, the germs would have found an almost embarrassing choice in the selection of a new host.

Both George and I had secreted our money in our shirts which we slept in. We were notified to be on hand for an early breakfast, for the steamer was scheduled to "sail at daylight," a bit of stock advice which presumably is always given steerage passengers so they can be got on board and "under the hatches" before those who travel above the "Plimsoll mark" are ready to come on board. She actually got away just before dark.

The ship was riding at anchor in the Mersey. The steerage passengers went out to her on a tender, or two or three tenders. Everybody was in readiness long before transportation for the trip to the dock was available. No one planned to be left behind, though later some may have wished for the rest of their lives that this had happened. We finally left the "hotel" in wagons, the baggage piled in the bottom and the passengers given the privilege of riding on top of their trunks, bags, and bundles. One passenger who was riding on our wagon wore slippers; they were possibly the latest idea in his home town, but he lost one of them "overboard" as the wagon

"One family was particularly interesting."

jolted over the cobblestone pavements. He arrived at the dock wearing only one of his "late style" slippers. The scene at the dock and on the decks of the tenders was what I believe an artist would call "picturesque." Presently we were berthed alongside the *Alaska*. It was all very thrilling. A gangplank was put up and the passengers invited to come on board. They crowded to the foot of the gangplank as though they feared that accommodations would all be taken before they got on board. Judging by the hordes on the tenders, there was plenty of ground for their fears, but they had never occupied steerage quarters on an Atlantic liner and perhaps did not even know how many sardines can be packed in a can. They received no help from the ship's staff. The stewards and waiters, who are usually so much in evidence to help first cabin passengers with their belongings—and receive suitable tips for their interest—did not appear anxious to tackle the heavy bundles of the emigrants. They may also have suspected that the emigrants had not yet acquired a good working knowledge of the Baedeker schedules.

Most of the passengers on the tenders appeared to be from continental Europe. One family was particularly interesting. A very shaggy-headed male appeared to be the father and husband. The mother, viewed biologically, was a marvel; she should have worn a blue ribbon as a mark of her physical fitness. Several very robust children completed the family group. The father led the procession up the gangplank—a good test of its safety. He carried a huge bundle in a 12x12 piece of canvas or duck tied by the four corners. The bundle, while it could have been lowered through the hatchway of the *Alaska,* or possibly have gone through the doorway of a boxcar, would certainly have needed some "breaking down" before it could have been taken through the entrance of a passenger coach. The family staggered up the gangplank, carrying everything the clan had accumulated since the time of the "Flood." The cargo—it could hardly be termed baggage—had been distributed among the members of the family in proportion to their size and strength. While the father had the largest and probably the heaviest bundle, the mother carried what would have been a good load for a camel. The children fell in line with their loads; possibly it had all been carefully rehearsed before they left the Ukraine, or from wherever they came. The last one in line was a chubby little fellow of about my age at the time Bundy built the Topping teahouse. His share of the family load was limited to carrying a vessel such as was then, and still is, commonly used in English bedrooms. The art of enameling on iron had been in practice long enough for manufacturers to make some interesting experiments. This particular article was enameled in an irregular pattern or design: on the outside in bright blue and white; the inside had originally been white. It no doubt was considered by its maker as quite a masterpiece of art and apparently was fully appreciated by its present possessors. But its sharply contrasting colors made it very conspicuous. It might have been seen on the horizon at a greater distance than the ship—a wonderful color scheme for lighthouses and beacons. The little boy was wholly unconscious of the prominent rôle which had been assigned him. But I am sure his memory was as faithfully recording the experiences of the day as did mine the various happenings in my life when I was his age. Forty years later when our little hero had achieved the success which such little boys almost invariably do achieve—most likely with such an initial training he became a Kohler or a Crane—and on some occasion after he had risen to prominence and a position of civic leadership and his fellow townsmen were gathered to honor him, as he stepped to the front of the platform to acknowledge their plaudits, it may have been noticed that there was a catch in his throat and a moment of hesitation which would be attributed to emotion, but which in reality was caused by a mental vision of himself walking up the gangplank of the *Alaska* carrying that service-stained sky blue and white enameled cast-iron pot. He would wonder if any in his audience had seen him at that time and recognized him now. A child should be protected from mental scars as it would be from physical disfigurement.

My parents had not felt so badly about my leaving since I was not going so far and would meet the cousins at the end of the journey. I had parted with my parents so many times that I was not so impressed as I otherwise would have been. I had their assurance that I would be cared for, whatever happened, if I could reach home. It was seventeen years before I again saw them.

The *Alaska* steamed out of the Mersey. We were shown our quarters. We had each paid four pounds for the voyage. This was one pound more than was demanded for the passage on most ships but was justified partly on account of the ship's greater speed and also because she did not carry live cattle on her east-bound trips as many of the ships did in space which was allotted to steerage passengers on the west-bound voyage. I did not wish to travel on a cattle boat; there might be an odd bull in the cabin which had forgotten to go on shore at Liverpool. All the single men were stowed, and "stowed" is the right word, in one large cabin—large by comparison with some cabins but small indeed for the horde which occupied it. The cabin was below the water line and in the bows of the ship, strictly the business end during rough weather. The berths were strips of canvas about sixteen inches in width, stretched on iron frames. These berths were four deep, the lower one having about six inches floor clearance. The two next above were far enough apart to permit the occupant only a horizontal position; the top one was far enough below the deck to permit sitting up in a crouched position. They were constructed on narrow aisles; entrance was from the end. There was, however, but one aisle for two rows of berths. They were like the aisles on the cattle boat but narrower. Passengers crawling in head first would have been head to head with the occupant of the berth which had its outlet in the next aisle, but they did not lie that way. It would have been "impractical"; they turned in their narrow quarters with their heads to the open end. This was necessary in case of sickness which, like the purity of the much advertised soap, was in the proportion of about 99 44/100 per cent.

By some coincidence, or because the stewards did not wish to separate such a bucolic couple, George and I had adjoining berths in an upper tier. This had both its advantages and disadvantages. While no one could, as it were, throw his dinner at us, the air in the upper berths was very bad. There were no partitions separating the berths. We lay in rows like the terrible pictures of the dead after some major catastrophe. We had brought no blankets, and none were provided. For that matter, in particular in the upper berths, the air was stiflingly hot; air conditioning had not yet been developed. And anyway the passengers could get all the fresh air they needed by going on deck. Air in the cabin—when any—was supplied from ventilators in the same way as on the cattle boat, but either there were not enough of these or they did not function properly. Under such conditions, men who never before in their lives had parted with food when once they had swallowed it, now seemed anxious to find something they had eaten before they left Poland.

Among the passengers from the continent were many Jews who evidently entertained some orthodox ideas about hair and whiskers. Many of the men wore long coats to their heels and whiskers to their knees. Their whiskers were so loaded with food droppings that one could conclude that they carried crumbs from every birthday cake which had marked for them the passage of time.

We stopped at Queenstown; a tugboat came alongside with a bargeload of passengers. The stewards hustled them up the gangplank, for when once on her way, the *Alaska* showed no disposition to loiter. She had that greyhound reputation to maintain, and she apparently was being given the same kind of encouragement that the owner of the *Julia May* had been so free with. One elderly man could not find his ticket, and some of the stewards helped him in the search. They probably had never heard of Mr. Smith who distinguished himself in my native village, but they were familiar with his method. They took off the passenger's clothes and found the ticket in his shirt. He dashed up the gang-plank with his clothes under his arm.

Among these Irish passengers was a very tall raw-boned youth of eighteen or twenty years of age. Steerage accommodations on the *Alaska* must have been at a premium, for a small space which, following the curve in the ship's bow at the end of our tier of berths and which was only about eight inches wide at one end, had been fitted with a strip of canvas cut to fit, and this plan was no doubt followed in the spaces below. This Irish lad was assigned this limited space at the end of our tier as his berth. It was wholly impossible for him to stow himself in such narrow quarters. The iron framework did not permit of "borrowing" from the adjoining berth. As a more "seasoned" traveler, I felt it to be my duty to help the unfortunate lad. The berth on one side was occupied by my former schoolmate—I did not consider him seasoned; the one on my other side had as its occupant a north of England man who talked a most terrible brogue. He looked intelligent, so I enlisted his help in forming a committee to protest the treatment of the Irish boy. "All right," he said, "let us interview the passenger." When we found the lad and finally made him understand through our dialects—Yorkshire, Southern Ireland, and East Anglian—what we were trying to do for him, he did not manifest any interest or appear to be at all disturbed over the fact that he had no sleeping quarters. He was on board and no doubt, in the absence of any compass in the steerage quarters, he would conclude that he was headed for America. What more could he desire? My committeeman was disgusted and remarked: "That beggar could sleep on a clothesline." We were then in the position that defenders of the oppressed have often found themselves in; the oppressed did not know that they were being oppressed, until someone, usually with ulterior motives, told them about it.

I have forgotten, if I ever knew, what the tonnage of the *Alaska* was, but she was not a large ship compared with even the moderate-sized liners of today. It was stated that she carried upward of thirty-eight hundred passengers. This may be an exaggeration, but anyone traveling in the steerage on that voyage could not have been convinced that the number was less than double that figure. When the ticket agent sold my traveling companion his ticket, he gratuitously gave him a little advice. "Look out for sharps," he had said. "Sharps" in those days were what are now known as "slickers." The first "sharp" that George met was the agent himself, who sold what he did not deliver in the way of accommodations. "Sharps" were supposed to live by picking off the "flats." There are more "flats" these days, and "sharps" make a better or easier living. George tried to pass this advice on to me, but I told him I had had experience and did not want anything which was being given away. We had not been long on board the *Alaska* before we found out that we were the "flats," all right. In purchasing our tickets we should have asked for a diagram showing our staterooms, bath, etc. Also, this would have given the location of the lounge, smoking room, and dining saloon. The steerage cabin berths on the *Alaska* were hardly to be described as berths. There was no dining room; we were fed on the open "tween decks," almost like a lot of hogs in Mr. Pilcher's hogyard. The lounge was the same deck except that when the weather was tolerable we could go on the upper deck.

Furthermore, we found that the ship did not supply any dishes, cups, or cutlery. The stewards, however, stood ready to correct that oversight; they were the "sharps" of that particular occasion. We each bought a tin plate, a tin cup, a spoon, a three-pronged fork, and a knife. These were all of ten-cent-store quality but sold over the dollar counter. These "tools" had been sold and resold every trip since the steamer was first commissioned. We could, had we known, have dispensed with both the knife and the fork as we had nothing but spoon food on the trip. We must surely have sometimes had something other than hash but we had hash so frequently that anything else which may have been served, and also the memory of it, are buried under that hash. The hash was composed for the most part of potatoes with an occasional small cube of meat which went to those who were properly equipped with horseshoes or rabbits' feet to curry such favors.

The meals were served on the "tween decks." The stewards would appear bringing buckets of hash; other stewards carried buckets of coffee. They usually selected the forehatch as the point or place of distribution. They would deposit their buckets on the hatches which were about knee high from the deck. Then with dippers they would fill the extended plates with hash and the cups with coffee. This at least was intended to be the procedure under properly ordered conditions, but the self-help idea, rather than order, prevailed on the good ship *Alaska*. No sooner would the stewards deposit their buckets of hash on the hatch, than they were rushed by the hungry hoard who dipped their tin cups in the "fluid" hash and transferred it next to their tin plates. They would then assail the coffee buckets, dipping their cups on which a rather negligible element of fat from the hash had "set." If the coffee was hot enough it would dissolve the grease on the cup which rose to the surface making it difficult to tell which was hash and which was coffee. Other stewards followed, bringing huge baskets of very large rolls of bread. They never got as far as the hatch with their baskets; since both their hands were engaged in carrying the baskets, they were entirely helpless to stage any defence, and their baskets were emptied under their eyes and noses. Sometimes the hash and coffee stewards would attempt to restore order, or perhaps it would be more proper to state they would try to establish it. They would fill their dippers with hash which they threw in the faces of their attackers or, at close range, they beat them over their heads with the dippers. But the hardy emigrants were not easily deterred. They had "backing" in the form of the crowd pushing them into the fray. My orthodox fellow passengers trailed their sacred whiskers in the hash. They would have their share at any cost short of losing a whisker. They intended to "get on" in the new world to which they were bound and were working hard to break down their natural and inherent bashfulness. The stewards usually continued bringing hash, coffee, and rolls as long as the "demand" lasted. There is no doubt but that everyone would have received all they needed, or at least all that was good for them, had they manifested less greed.

Every forenoon all the steerage passengers were assembled on the upper deck. Those too sick to walk much had been carried out and up. The cabin was then given a thorough washing with the fire hose and certainly with no place to be "sick" but on the deck or floor of the cabin, this was none too often. After the cabin was scrubbed with brooms, whole barrels of chloride of lime would be scattered around, the fumes of which would choke the passengers if they returned to the cabin too soon. Germs were not given even a handicapped chance on board the *Alaska*. I don't know how these sanitary arrangements could have been carried out had it been too rough for the passengers to go on deck, but fortunately there was nothing worse than a good fresh and particularly cold wind which continued throughout the voyage.

One day we were steaming along with a strong breeze from the north; the air was piercingly cold, a heavy swell was rolling. The *Alaska* had no bulwarks above the foredeck. These had probably been omitted to enable her to better clear herself when steaming into a heavy sea and putting her bows under. Some staunch iron railings served to keep the passengers from going over the side. Among the many perversities of human nature is the one which passengers on an ocean liner display in going to the weather side of the ship when they just must part with their last—and perhaps the next to the last also—feed of hash. With no bulwarks to interrupt the flow, the partly digested and completely soured hash was blown back on the deck and on the passengers' clothes. No one appeared to be interested in teaching them to go to the lee side. And signs in twenty different languages would not have meant much, for probably the majority of them could not

"The air was piercingly cold, a heavy swell was rolling."

read. On this particular morning the entire steerage passenger list were assembled shivering on the deck. As the deck was full of people, many could find nothing to hold on to but each other. Presently the ship gave an unusually heavy roll. Some of them lost their balance, and they clutched wildly at others. The whole mass collapsed on the hash-coated deck and slid to the side of the ship, mopping up as they went back and forth across the deck. Such an aggregation of filth and misery as these wretched passengers represented was probably never before nor since set afloat under the British flag.

The *Alaska* made the run—and this was in 1891—in seven days and a few hours. In forty-five years the time has not been greatly reduced except by a few modern "Greyhounds of the Atlantic." We landed at Castle Garden. How romantic the name sounds, but no other name could have been more inappropriate. The passengers were all as eager to get on shore as they had been to get on board. So far they had not found any experience which they wished to prolong. At the first signal they rushed as they had done for the hash and coffee. The jobs, no doubt, were for those who arrived first. No wonder they had fought for the bread rolls. As they marched on shore, many of them carried in addition to their huge bundles of baggage, large packages, and some of the more enterprising, and perhaps more fully advised, carried gunny sacks filled with the bread rolls. Enough food to take them to San Francisco or back to Warsaw. But where had they secreted the rolls during the voyage? It could have been done only by using their berths for storage while they stood like horses and slept in the aisles. Why did the ship's owners permit this wholesale pilferage? Perhaps they charged the loss to advertising, or it may have been an early day manifestation of what is now commonly called "chiseling" on the price of the ticket. They were coming to a land of plenty but "safety first" was an age-old slogan with them long before Columbus was born. The outward evidences of piety as expressed in long coats, uncombed—for fear of breaking one holy strand—hair and whiskers, was no handicap to the acquisition of useful material things by the descendants of Abraham, Isaac, and Jacob, who composed a substantial percentage of the passenger list.

On shore we encountered the immigration authorities. Their attitude was widely different from that of those who usually represent that department of the Government today. They did not challenge us with menacing looks and unanswerable questions about where were you born and what your mother's name was before her marriage, and so forth. In the case of George and myself, they rushed forward like "hotel greeters" to meet us; no questioning the warmth of their welcome. They did not give us time to answer the few questions they asked us but slapped us on the back to get us out of the way. Today I shiver when I meet one for fear that it shall be proved that I am a "man without a country" who can neither land here nor return to the place he so recently left.

The place was divided with high fences made of 1x4 lumber. We could see all around but could not get out of the particular corral in which we had been herded. None of the long-whiskered fellows were put in our corral. They were not going to Michigan and, as for Utah, "no indeed." They probably stayed in New York and are there today with their whiskers, by this time long enough to tuck in their boots. We spent the entire day in the corral and could not find out why we were detained. Possibly a dispute among the railroad officials about the division of the "loot." All the different corrals converged on a large booth, where food was sold. We looked the stock over. There was nothing such as we had been raised on, but we finally bought a very large brown sausage—which shone as though it were oiled or varnished—and a loaf of bread nearly a yard long. It was made of something to which we were not accustomed, probably rye flour. The two ends of the sausage were tied together. George hung it on his arm. Not finding any other place to sit, we finally sat on the floor of the enclosure and ate our first meal in America. What we could not eat we tucked unwrapped under our arms and awaited the next event.

There had been a great deal of squabbling among some of the passengers. Friends had come to meet them and talked with them through the 1x4 fences. They may have been "picture brides" or "grooms" who did not measure up to the claims of the photograph, but who would after such an experience? One corral, from the viewpoint of future American citizens, held a very undesirable crowd, some of whom looked actually villainous. I have no doubt but that the inspectors could spot those "not wanted" as readily as a bank teller could a wooden dollar.

It was getting dark when we were finally marched out and put in a Delaware and Lackawanna day coach. The cargo had evidently been equitably divided at last among the different carriers. Soon our train was assembled and ready for the dash westward. It was warm and comfortable in the car. We had had an exciting day. I fell asleep but was awakened by a nudge from my companion's elbow. "Look what you missed by going to sleep." He had a carton of candy which he called "sweets." He had already opened it and was munching the contents. He offered me some.

"Where did you get the sweets?" I asked him.

"A man gave them to me; he gave everybody a package; you'd have got one had you been awake." This generosity seemed unusual even for America, of which we both held high hopes. But it was no surprise to George. He said: "Why wouldn't they give us sweets? Didn't they give each of us a Bible?" Our experience earlier in the day was not new to me. I had found people before who were giving away Bibles and very frequently giving away selected parts of the book in the form of tracts, but sweets —never. Soon, our benefactor appeared picking up his wares. None of the packages, other than George's, had been opened. The assorted crowd of aliens, with which every seat in the car was filled, had probably received "presents" before and later found that there was usually a string attached. When the vendor reached our seat, he said: "A shilling, please." He thought we had not been on shore long enough to know what was meant by a quarter. George knew what was meant by a shilling; he could interpret that into a half day's hard work. The ticket agent was right; there were "sharps" and they were getting too thick. George stood up in the aisle of the lurching car; he raised his fists in an attitude of assault. The candy seller backed out of reach. The different Continentals showed interest; they evidently understood the "science of assault" and were expectant. I placed myself between George and his intended victim. I paid the man the quarter, which so enraged George that I narrowly escaped a thrashing myself.

I parted with George for what proved to be forever. Somewhere in Michigan he took the remainder of the rye bread and sausage to sustain him till he reached Utah. He was without money; the four-foot ticket had taken almost his last penny. I gave him ten dollars; a few weeks later he sent me eleven dollars in payment. Thirty-six years later a business trip took me by motor to Salt Lake City. I stopped at the small town to which George had been billed. I found his widow and his nine surviving children. I learned that George had joined the Mormon Church and nine years previously had gone to the Mormon heaven. His friend who had encouraged him to emigrate was still living and told me the sad story of George's life in Utah. For a long time he had "enjoyed" but indifferent health. He had never been back to his native village nor any place farther away than Salt Lake City. He had lived in a fertile little valley at the base of the Wasatch Mountains, which almost all around towered into the sky, but at times he must have longed for the open country of East Anglia, the chimes of its many church bells, and the songs of the meadow larks. Poor George had deserved more in this world, and perhaps more than a Mormon heaven could promise in the next. I returned to Salt Lake City. At the hotel I could not sleep; it was all so inexpressibly sad.

I had arrived in Grand Rapids via the Detroit, Grand Haven and Milwaukee Railroad. The name reads like a transcontinental system, but it operated only from Detroit to Milwaukee and made the last lap of that short run as a ferry service across Lake Michigan. My half cousin, Mrs. Fisher, made me welcome at her home. Her family consisted of her mother, whose surname I bore, and her husband, an employee of one of the furniture factories. An only son had died. The Fisher family showed me great kindness. My half cousin, John Youell, who was quite well to do, also took an interest in me. I started out to look for a job, and when I was just about ready to continue my journey to British Columbia, I secured one as a carpenter's laborer on the railroad which had brought me to town at a wage of one dollar and twenty cents a day. It was now June and quite warm. My work was the heavy inexpert labor such as carrying ties and bridge timbers, digging for foundations, and sometimes swinging an axe or running a crosscut saw for days at a time. The men in the gang were all Germans as also was the foreman. They conversed in their mother tongue. The life was not very thrilling, my first thrill coming when, after five weeks, the foreman, speaking English so there would be no danger of his being misunderstood, told me my services were no longer needed. Pressed for a reason, he explained that I was too stupid to perform such work as carrying ties and digging holes.

I found more jobs; sometimes they did not last

long, and if they did, I did not. I worked on farms. I worked at street grading but always I quickly worked myself out of a job. After being "relieved" once, I never again tried to argue with my employers when they said they no longer "needed" me. I preferred to give myself the benefit of that very faint doubt. At the street grading work I was assigned to holding the scraper, a small sort of scoop which was drawn by two horses. I had scooped up a lot of the North Sea while on the *Bessie Pepper* and other similar craft, but this was different. I held the scraper at an angle which sank it in the earth where the horses could not pull it. Sometimes the blade hit a rock and I would be suddenly catapulted over to the horses' heels. My teamster did not manifest any impatience—he was working by the day—but the foreman soon spotted me and told me he no longer "needed" me. If he were to make a profit on his contract, I realized that he did not "need" many of my caliber on the job. I had not done much toward giving Grand Rapids its street system. I worked some at harvesting. Farmers cannot afford to be too particular at harvesttime when help is scarce. I also picked apples, a job I liked; but this of course could not last but a short time. I ate and slept in many different places and had many different but no profitable experiences.

In the fall of 1891, my cousin John advised me that I should try to get an inside job, for Michigan winters were usually quite severe. He suggested that, since I was a teetotaler, I would make a good bartender; that such an idiosyncracy as being a teetotaler would appeal to any saloonkeeper. He would not need to worry that I would drink all the profits of the trade. He would only need to keep his eye on the cash register to be sure I rang up all the sales. This profession or trade had been reviewed in my *Thousand Ways to Make a Living* but apparently was not very highly regarded, the work in England for the most part being done by maids whose employment depended more on their good looks than on any ability they might possess or lack. Besides, I did not like the smell of beer or liquor and knew nothing whatever about the "stock." I told my cousin John that all things being equal I was disposed to give hard work the preference. He then suggested that I try to get a job with Charley Chadwick, who had some greenhouses and a truck farm. I went out to the Chadwick farm, an eighty-acre truck farm just south of the city limits. Charley had a small new house and a very charming wife who was just my age, twenty-three, while Charley was two years my senior. He said he knew my cousin John and held him in high regard, that he appreciated my calling to see him, but at that season there was little or nothing doing on a truck farm. If I would come out in the spring, he was sure he could find me a job. I had learned a lot since I left England about how to get jobs but had yet to learn how to keep one. I was developing some of the characteristics of those hash-pilfering emigrants on the *Alaska*. Get your eye on what you want whether it is a bucket of hash or a job and then keep going. It was no doubt Charley's intention to dismiss me for at least a few months, but I had other ideas. I finally sold myself for eight dollars a month, my board, and a room in the new house. It was, however, with the distinct understanding that during the winter months there would not be much to do —some work in the greenhouses and some outside, for there were some jobs which could be done even during the winter. To fill in odd moments there was a huge woodpile waiting to be sawed into suitable stove lengths. This association yielded a good deal of profit, though not in a monetary way. True, my winter working schedule did not look as though it could be greatly expanded during the summer months, for I commenced firing the greenhouses at five a.m. and gave them a last refuelling at nine at night. It was a great help to be thrown with educated people. I had had many different associates since I had left home ten and a half years previous, but most of them were not the types that provided any mental stimulus. Mrs. Chadwick was very kind to me and tried to help me in different ways. I was in that unfinished state where a lot of help could be used in my development. She introduced me to her friends; they were staunch friends or they would have resented the introductions. She lent me books which, however, I had not much time to read. She tried to correct my speech and grammar; others even more devoted have since worked to that end with no encouraging results.

In the spring Charley raised me to twelve dollars monthly, later to sixteen, then twenty, the latter being top wages at that time. Mrs. Chadwick served good meals; everything was lovely, but I did not feel well. I had not felt well at any time since I arrived in Michigan but was told that I would feel better when I became acclimated. It began to appear that I might not live to attain that condition. I visited a number of doctors; they had not before appeared to me to be a very necessary class. In turn, they looked me over, wrote out prescriptions, charged me a uniform fee of two dollars—they must have had a code of "fair prices"—and told me if I were not better, which I am sure they knew I would not be, to come back in two weeks. In two weeks, the medicine which had cost sometimes seventy-five cents, at other times a dollar—the prescription druggists evidently had not yet adopted a code of "uniform prices"—was exhausted and I went back but never twice to the same doctor. If a man did not know his business, which I concluded none of them did, why see him a second time? And so far, all my doctors had been equally unable to diagnose my case.

One evening during the latter part of August when we had had one of those busy days which Charley had predicted as far back as the previous November, and when I felt particularly played out, I decided to go to town and try to find a doctor at night. A walk of a mile or so brought me to the end of the car line on Burton Avenue. The cars ran now and then—mostly then. A small building had been erected at the end of the car line and was then occupied by a not much needed grocery store. An apartment over the store, no doubt intended for the grocer's occupancy, was in the possession of a doctor who had a small sign extending from the stairway. The grocer doubtless was sleeping under the counter until he had his business established. All doctors looked alike to me, and none of them looked like life savers at that. Why go to town when here was a doctor right out in the country? I ascended the stairs and was greeted by a young man who admitted that he was the doctor. "How can I serve you?" he asked. I told him I wanted him to tell me what ailed me. He said: "Take off your clothes and I'll examine you." This I did. He tested my heart and lungs, then standing off and looking at me, he exclaimed: "Your heart is all right, your lungs are perfect but, oh, how thin you are!" I was indeed thin; anyone could have counted my ribs from the opposite side of Canal Street, Grand Rapids. He added, "The trouble with you is the climate.

You are full of malaria. You had better go back where you came from." My brogue was still sufficiently pronounced for anyone to tell that I came from "somewhere," even though they could not tell where "somewhere" was.

I asked him: "How about going the other way?" To this he replied: "I don't know where the other way is, but I am sure you would make no mistake going there." I put on my clothes and asked him how much I owed him for the advice. But he told me that I did not owe him anything, and extending his hand, as he shook mine, he said: "Goodbye, and good luck to you." I have been guilty of much ingratitude in my life. I forgot the name of this fine young doctor as I have forgotten the name of my kind-hearted Boston landlady, but I acted promptly on his advice.

Professional advertisers or those who seek to advise advertisers claim that it is no use to advertise unless you do it all the time. British Columbia may have continued to advertise all the time but not in all places. Not much was heard about British Columbia in Grand Rapids, but a great deal could be heard about the wonders of Seattle. I resigned my job—about the first job I had had a chance to resign since I landed in America. In all other instances my employer had beat me to it by telling me he no longer "needed" me.

I made the matter of "going the other way" the

first order of business. I went to a newsstand to procure a Seattle paper, but they were sold out. Seattle papers were in great demand, but the dealer had a Portland *Oregonian,* and Portland was only two hundred miles from Seattle. Any good boom could be felt that short distance, and anyway the ticket was the same price and a longer ride for my money. I bought the *Oregonian* and turned to the "Help Wanted Male" column. The help was wanted but not to fill good jobs; rather, to send their laundry to certain laundries and to eat at specified restaurants. I bought a ticket for Portland. I paid thirty-two dollars for the ticket and as it included my berth on the sleeper, it seemed like a lot of transportation for the price. Had I received the thirty-two dollars in place of parting with that amount, the ticket would have been no great bargain. The route was by the Canadian Pacific Railway. I bid goodbye to the Chadwicks, to the few friends I had made, to my cousins, and the dear old aunt. Mr. Fisher, my cousin's husband, said: "George, if you are going to Portland on the Canadian Pacific Railway, you must go through Tacoma. I have a nephew living there, Will Cunnington, who used to live in Kansas; I have not heard from him direct for twenty years. Can't you stop off at Tacoma and look him up?" I was willing to stop off anywhere to see anybody. Mr. Fisher added: "I heard he was running a bakeshop."

I left Grand Rapids by rail to Benton Harbor, by boat from that point to Chicago, by day coach from Chicago to Winnipeg, where the "sleeper" would be waiting. The sleeper was there all right, and the simplicity of its arrangements almost equaled the steerage quarters on the *Alaska,* but the beds were harder. On the *Alaska* I slept on a strip of canvas; on the sleeper I slept on the boards. There were no curtains or partitions. The French would, I think, describe this manner of sleeping as *en famille.* Nothing in English would describe it. Fumigation, if it ever took place, should have been most effective. If there was a flea in the car, for lack of any place to hide, he would have had to stand out in the open and take his punishment like a man. There was no diner on the train, but it stopped for meals at specified stations indicated on the time table. I tried the dining room once but, owing to the rates, the station lunch counters the rest of the time. Some of the passengers acted as though they were sorry for me; they probably thought I was a tuberculosis victim who was trying to travel faster than the dread disease. There was one young lady on the train who seemed to be particularly sorry for me but in the end she must have married the other fellow.

I arrived in Tacoma in the evening, and ate dinner at a Japanese restaurant for fifteen cents, which seemed reasonable. I spent the night at the Halstead House, a small frame building, and the next morning started to look for Mr. Fisher's nephew. Tacoma then had a population of about thirty-five thousand. I found the nephew without any trouble and easily identified him by his likeness to his uncle. He was pleased to meet me and to have word from his uncle from whom he said he had not heard in twenty years. They probably had forgotten which one had written the last letter. However, when I mentioned the bakeshop, he seemed somewhat mortified. He said he had had his ups and downs, and rather more of the latter than the former, but he had never descended to the level of running a bakeshop. His business appeared to be that of going out in the country and buying loads of elderly chickens when they had lost interest in egg laying and their owners had lost interest in feeding them. These he brought in alive and killed them as orders came in. His wife helped him at this and would no doubt have been just as willing to help him in a bakeshop as in picking feathers from fowls. In selling a housewife a fowl, I noticed that Mr. Cunnington had one standard piece of advice for the housewife, intended, I am sure, to save embarrassment on both sides. "This is a nice fowl, Madam, but put it on early." In his shop was a scale on which he weighed coops of chickens. I weighed myself on this and was shocked to find that I weighed only one hundred and forty pounds. Mr. Cunnington manifested a kindly interest in me, asked what I had done in the "Old

Country" and what I planned to do in Portland. When I told him of my experience in the fisheries, he said he knew a man who kept books for a newly organized fish company in Tacoma. They might have an opening; he would drive me to the dock and introduce me to his friend, the bookkeeper. This he did.

The friend said, after I had told him of my ten years on the North Sea: "I think the president of our company would like to meet you, if you can spare the time." I had not yet learned to place much value on my time and offered to give the president all he needed of it in which to interview me. Mr. Cunnington then left me, suggesting that I return to the chicken shop when the interview was ended. I was then shown into the very nicely furnished office of the president and formally introduced. The president was a genial-appearing man who said he was glad to meet me and actually looked as though he meant it. The company had been very recently organized, and no doubt all its stockholders as well as its officers were bursting with enthusiasm over their bright prospects. "I understand," he said, "that you have had experience in deep-sea fishing in European waters." I told him about my ten years in the work. I think that all the president knew about fish was that it appeared immediately above the entree on the bills of fare. He responded with the remark, "I would like to invite you to make a trip on my steamer to the fishing grounds on this coast and advise me whether you think any of the methods in use in European waters are, in your opinion, applicable to the industry here." He went on to state: "There are very nice quarters on the boat, and as my guest you will be shown every consideration. The boat is in port today, and if you wish to go on the next trip I will have a letter of introduction to the Captain prepared." I told him I would take the letter at this time. The letter was dictated and signed, then handed to me with a reiteration of his assurance that as his guest every consideration would be shown me and that he would await my report with interest. I went along the dock to where it had been indicated the steamer was moored. For a steamer she was disappointingly small—not more than one hundred tons. I found the Captain, an elderly man with a sort of "Jawn" twang in his speech. I handed him the letter of introduction, which he read with one eye while he looked me over with the other. Presently he finished the letter and carefully refolding it in its former creases, he handed it to me with the question, "Are you a sailor?" The letter had mentioned the ten years' experience but I told him: "Yes, I am a sailor; I have a mate's certificate." This he quickly assured me would not be needed, but that the boat was short a deck hand— forty-five dollars a month and board; he could offer me that berth. I did not hesitate in saying: "You have shipped a deck hand, sir." He told me we would leave at six in the morning. He might have said one in the morning with no danger of leaving me behind. He had not said: "We will set sail at six," the term to which I had been accustomed, because he had a steamboat.

I was at the dock ahead of time by the fastest clock in town. Promptly at six we released the moorings and steamed out into the Sound. I then had opportunity to learn of whom the crew consisted. There was first the "Jawn-voiced" Captain, the mate who was an Englishman, a chief engineer. The chief engineer had a fireman, but the second engineer fired and also ran the engines. An efficiency expert would no doubt have eliminated the fireman entirely. There were two deck hands, of whom I was privileged to be one, and the cook. I had not been a very important member of the crew when I was cook on the *Eclipse* but I soon learned that this cook had an entirely different status. The provisions I had had at my command could have been enumerated on one's fingers. The cook on our steamer had everything which he and an apparently well-qualified meat and grocery salesman could think of from which to prepare meals. As soon as we left the dock, breakfast was served in a small galley on the after part of the boat. The Captain, mate, and the engineers had the first sitting in the "dining room." Space was too limited to admit

(241)

more than four at a service. I was given a seat at the second or third table, when only Steve the fireman who went in with me and I remained to be fed.

Steve was wearing blue overalls and a snuff-colored shirt without sleeves. He was a bit grimy from his efforts to raise enough steam to last while he ate his breakfast. A counter extended across the small galley. Steve and I were seated on one side, the cook stood on the opposite side with his range beyond. The cook was a somewhat corpulent person. He did not do anything but cook, which left him plenty of time in which to eat and rest. The cook turned when we seated ourselves and, leaning heavily on his outspread palms, he addressed himself to Steve. This was most fortunate. Embarrassment for both the cook and myself would have been the result had he first spoken to me. My ears must have unconsciously moved forward a little when the cook spoke, for he said in very mild and respectful tones: "What do you wish for breakfast?" Never before had I heard such a remark on anything afloat, but to Steve it was quite evidently everyday language. For a few moments he was undecided, acting as though a Delmonico bill of fare had been placed in his hands. He threw back his head and, looking at the deck above, apparently finding it difficult to decide what he would have for his morning meal, he drawled: "Oh—er, give me a steak and a couple of eggs."

The cook questioned, "Hot cakes?"

"Oh—er, give me a steak and a couple of eggs."

"Yeah, hot cakes and coffee," was Steve's reply.

The cook edged along the counter till he stood balancing himself on his hands before me. "What will you have for breakfast?" he repeated. Clutching the edge of the counter to help maintain an attitude of ease and indifference, I said: "I'll take the same." Soon he placed our orders before us: each a large steak, two fried eggs on a small platter by the side, fried potatoes, a pile of hot cakes, a can of syrup, and the coffee. He watched us eat as though he were hoping for repeat orders, which this time at least were not forthcoming.

I went out on deck. The skipper, mate, and chief engineer were discussing the probabilities of the next meal. When the mate was able to leave that interesting subject, he turned to me. I was assigned to his watch. I spent a good part of my time when on duty at the wheel, but anything easier than standing at the wheel of a small steamer running in smooth water would certainly be the act of lying in bed.

Dinner was served—a royal meal including everything from soup to, but not including, nuts. For supper, another royal banquet. I was taking life very easy, leaning on the wheel, when at about ten o'clock the mate entered the pilothouse and took the wheel from me. "Go to the galley and prepare some coffee for me," he said.

"Yes, sir." Soon I reported back. "Your coffee is

ready, sir." He was gone for some twenty minutes when he returned and, pushing back the sliding door of the pilothouse, he entered wiping his mouth with the back of his hand. He relieved me of the wheel remarking: "You can go to the galley and have some coffee and what you wish to eat." I felt a little shy on my first visit to the galley on my own account. There were tiers of cases of canned fruit stacked across the after end of the galley. The cook had taken the sides off the boxes and the fruit appeared like a display on a grocer's shelves. They bore bright attractive labels with pictures of apricots, peaches, and pears, and were marked, "Cutting's California Canned Fruit." Certainly, as I soon learned, Mr. Cutting knew his business. I fried some eggs, looked in the icebox, which was filled with steaks and chops evidently in readiness for more breakfasts for the fireman and me. It seemed to be the mate's regular habit, as I soon learned, to have a meal on each night watch. It soon became my irregular habit to have a meal whenever I could escape from the pilothouse long enough to cook one. I thought on my first visit to the galley that Cutting's California Canned Fruit was intended for special occasions but soon changed that decision to mean all occasions. With my pocketknife I would cut the end out of a large-sized can of apricots, peaches, or pears, which I ate while my steak was cooking. I received some sharp reprimands from the mate about my inattention to duty but I did not argue or even reply. Nothing short of violence on his part would have kept me out of that galley.

We returned in about a week with a cargo of fish —halibut which we took on from some Norwegians at Neah Bay. They were fishing in the vicinity of Cape Flattery. These convenient fishing grounds have, I believe, since that time been worked out. We took salmon from Indians working at the mouths of rivers and creeks along the Straits of Juan de Fuca and the Sound. I don't think the Indians received in payment anything which could be considered legal tender, for at that time one could usually buy a salmon uptown in Tacoma—from men who had wagonloads of them—for five cents each.

I felt obliged to report to the president of the company that, so far as my observation had extended on this first trip, none of the methods in use in "European waters" were applicable to the industry here. But when I called at the office I was advised that that gentleman had gone east to sell more stock in the company. He did not leave soon enough or travel fast enough, or he may not have been a good stock salesman. At any rate he failed to keep the company in operation, for on our return from the third trip the sheriff was among those waiting to welcome us. The company had become insolvent serving big steaks for breakfast with eggs on the side. The sheriff took charge of

(245)

the boat and cargo, mostly salmon worth five cents each if he moved fast enough to dispose of them before they spoiled. The boat was tied up. The whole venture, as I learned later, had not been well conceived. A large company operating in the middle western states, handling butter, eggs, poultry, etc., had opened a branch in Tacoma, the local supply of those products at that time not being equal to the demand. The officers and directors of the creamery company visited Tacoma and learned while there that among the varied resources of the state was an abundant supply of fish. They learned further that the fish was free for the taking. In Iowa and Minnesota they often bought butter and eggs at very low prices but they had never seen the time when those commodities were free for the taking. Here was a new and wonderful opportunity—a prime food commodity absolutely free. They organized the fish company and elected the president of their company to be the president of the new corporation and at the same time voted him a salary of ten thousand a year for his services in that capacity. The president did not know much more about fish than the fish knew of butter and eggs, but he knew what an additional ten thousand a year meant.

The surprising news of the free fish was sent to friends further east and they subscribed for stock. The steamer was acquired, a suitable plant hastily erected, but they went broke on free fish. My job was ended, wages being by some thoughtful provision of the law, a first lien on the company's assets. I was paid in full.

When I returned to the Cunnington chicken shop, I weighed myself again. I had been twenty-one days on the boat and had gained twenty-one pounds. The creditors should have sued me. I took a room at the Cunnington house, or rather a half interest in one. An employee of the railroad company who worked in the yards at night held the other half interest. In that way the bed was kept busy most of the time. But soon I secured a job at the Old Town Mill, a large lumber mill on the water front. Here I received thirty dollars—but earned sixty—a month, with the privilege of living in one of the company's shacks on the hill behind the mill. It took a good deal of my time going and coming from town to the mill, and I could not get there early enough for their six o'clock breakfast but had to provide that at my own expense. I therefore gave up my half interest in the bed at the Cunnington home and moved out to the mill occupying a shack with a Jew and a Norwegian. This is the only time in my experience that I have seen a Jew doing someone else out of a job of real hard work. The Jew was an interesting fellow. He had received a good education. He had been in many parts of the world and could relate his travels and experiences in an interesting manner. He never told us what had brought him to such lowly estate. He had probably been guilty of something which caused him to lose caste with his own people. If he had lost caste with the police, he had chosen a good spot to avoid them, for if they are still looking for him it will not have occurred to them to look for a Jew in a spot where the only activity was plain hard work. All Jews may not be smart but none of them are dumb enough to be found in such surroundings.

The Norwegian did not contribute much to the life of the shack. He was despondent, and his health was poor—or he thought it was, which would be an even worse condition. He had a quart bottle of medicine labeled, "Microbe Killer," from which he took frequent and copious doses. He might have convinced most anyone else but he could not have convinced the waiter who served our table that anything but overeating ailed him.

I stayed with the mill company for several weeks. The food was coarse, but there were no restrictions on the amount one could eat. Breakfast was served at six. I got along very well after the more substantial meal served at noon but I would almost expire before that time came. Breakfast always consisted of oatmeal mush and hot cakes. This food was quite acceptable but it lacked staying qualities when one was engaged in carrying lumber. At about eleven in the morning I would decide that next day I would eat a few additional hot cakes but though I ate all I could push behind my teeth, the feeling toward noon would be the same.

I heard that, on account of so many ships loading wheat, longshore work was plentiful, the men being paid fifty cents an hour. I resigned my job at the mill, bade my friends the Jew and the "Microbe Killer"-drinking Norwegian goodby.

Longshore work was plentiful, but the labor supply was fully commensurate. The work was closely unionized, and the fifty cents an hour compensation was rigidly adhered to, but the union members were given the preference in employment and also appeared to have the preference in selecting the jobs. The union, I found when I made application for membership, was a closed corporation, or a club with a full list. The best I could do was to go on the waiting list and wait for some of the members to die or be crippled so they could not work. This latter contingency was in the front rank of probabilities. I secured plenty of work; in fact, about all I was able to perform. My living expenses were low. I ate at the Japanese restaurant where I had had my first dinner. It was a popular place with the longshoremen, but I don't think the restaurant belonged to any union or they might have done better than selling meals for fifteen cents.

I had regained my half interest in the bed with the railroad worker. Sometimes I would work all day

(249)

and a good part of the night. Ships were always in a hurry—even if their crews were not—to get back to sea. On these occasions there would sometimes be some slight overlapping in bed service. I would retire in the early hours of the morning after fifteen or sometimes eighteen hours of good vigorous work on the docks or in the hold of a ship and when my partner would return from his night's work in the railroad yards, it would take real good arguments to convince me that it was time to get up.

Working in the mill and at longshore work did not permit me to add to my weight as I had done on the fish boat but it afforded a fine opportunity for proportionate muscular development. I weighed one hundred and forty pounds when I arrived in Tacoma. I eventually reached a peak of two hundred and ten pounds.

Tacoma is a lovely city with a fine climate and a magnificent view of the mountain, which they fondly and quite properly call Mount Tacoma though everyone else in the world may call it Mount Rainier.

In the early summer I left the water front to engage in business on my own account. I still had money which I had earned on the North Sea and which had been supplemented by my earnings as a longshoreman. My tastes were simple, and I had been able to earn six or seven dollars a day, most of which was added to my surplus. I earned more money than I needed to spend but I have never saved money. It is easier to make a dollar than to save a dime. Saving money requires a great deal of planning and consideration. Money can usually be "made" by an expenditure of effort, and making money is much more exhilarating than scheming for small savings. This was a most propitious time to engage in business. Depression was general, and Tacoma was at the sump of the depression, but everybody was feeling cheerful. The lowest spot is the bottom of anything.

In 1895 I met the "girl of girls." We were married in 1897 and lived happily ever after.

~~~~~~~~~~~~~~~~~~~~~~~~~~~~~~~~~~~~~~~
~~~~~~~~~~~~~~~~~~~~~~~~~~~~~~~~~~~~~~~
~~~~~~~~~~~~~~~~~~~~~~~~~~~~~~~~~~~~~~~

On a recent trip to England I again saw Jumbo. He had developed a disorder which prevented him from continuing on the trawlers, even had he been able to secure a berth, which, his age considered, was most unlikely. He stated that he had been having rather a hard time keeping himself alive. He was wearing a new—but for him—very much oversized suit, the pilot jacket of which came to his knees. He apologized for being so well dressed but said he had just taken delivery of the suit which he had bought on the installment plan, having paid a shilling down and a shilling whenever he could spare one until he had finally paid in enough to entitle him to a suit which had not been selected until the installments had been paid. This method of installment buying has features which place the merchant in a somewhat arbitrary position as to "adjustments and alterations." The installment method of this dealer was something in advance of the usual practice in this country where deliveries are made at the time of the sale and payments are arranged on the basis of a dollar down and a dollar a week during the remainder of the life of the purchaser.

Jumbo said at that time he had one year to go before he would be old enough to be eligible for the old age pension of ten shillings a week. The payment of this pension, from the way Jumbo explained it to me, was based entirely on the age of the applicant. Just prove that you are sixty-five and you are at once entered on the payroll. It all appeared very simple, but later reflection on my part convinced me that in Jumbo's case it might not be so easy. He would have to prove where he was born, and where would he go for that evidence? In fact, it would not be a very easy matter for him to prove that he had ever had any parents or that he had ever been born at all. This pension of ten shillings a week would mean for Jumbo, provided he was able to secure it, affluence for the rest of his life, and food costs in England are considerably higher than in the United States. People in America would think that ten shillings a week, or its American equivalent of ten dollars a month, had left them stranded out of sight of "affluence," but Jumbo had lived under other standards. One expense item common to many Americans which would have no place in Jumbo's budgetary figures would be that of cigarettes. He certainly had never developed that costly vice. Often have I noticed the nicotine-stained fingers of the panhandler. I have no doubt but that many of these "down but not outs" spend more money for cigarettes than Jumbo would have needed for food.

While on my different trips to England, I have tried to find as many as possible of my old shipmates. I have not found any who had achieved independence or anything approaching that condition. They had led lives of hardship without much in the way of rewards. The annual loss of life had continued to be heavy. Some had been drowned, others had died, some were already drawing the old age pension which, when a man and his wife were both living, would often be more than his average earnings had been. They were better off than they had been before in their lives; they had finally secured a "steady job," and on shore at that.

I talked with the skipper of a trawler which during the War had been armed, at his request, by the Government with a gun to defend him against attacks by submarines. Some one hundred of the Lowestoft trawlers had been sunk, the enemy's idea being to deprive the English of that source of food. They were not sunk with torpedoes, for that would have been too expensive, but were disposed of by notifying the crew to leave in their boat and come alongside the submarine. Two or three men from the submarine would then instruct the trawler's crew to row them to the craft they had just left when a time bomb would be placed in the hold and the submarine's men returned to their craft. The trawlers, after their vessel was blown up, were left to do the best they could, afloat in the middle of the North Sea in a small open boat. A new trawler would cost but seven or eight thousand dollars and torpedoes are expensive. The skipper told me that when a submarine came to the surface almost alongside his boat and, placing a German flag on a pole in a socket on the afterdeck, gave them the usual order to get out their boat and come alongside, he promptly removed the tarpaulin covering the gun and before the surprised submarine could submerge, had sent four shots through her which he surmised, on account of the close range, went through both sides of her hull. This man stated that his only previous contact with Germans had been usually with those who bought herring for export to that country previous to the War, since which they have not had any money with which to buy herring. His impression of them was that they were neither better nor worse than his own countrymen; that he had not realized until it was done what it meant to be the cause of the death of twenty or twenty-five men who were drowned like rats in a trap. He stated that the effect on him was sickening, but fortunately he never had to sink another. However, one old trawler actually sank seven submarines. When the Germans discovered these "mystery ships" they withdrew their submarines from that area.

A few years ago I took my wife to England to see the home where I was born. As a dwelling it looked wretchedly inadequate. We wandered down the garden behind the house. A feeble attempt was being made to grow some vegetables on the tiny strip of exhausted land. Crop rotation had probably not been well considered; soil analysis would have indicated a lack of every element necessary to the production of vegetables. It was untidy and unkempt. The marvelous privet hedge which had screened us, and generally effectively so, from the Topping gaze and what was more important to them, had as they supposed screened them from our eyes though it had permitted me to watch activities through the lower part, had been replaced with a fence made of odds and ends of rusted sheet iron, hard indeed to look at. The Topping blacksmith shop, while still used for the same purpose, was in a very propped-up and tumbled-down condition.

The Red Lion alone had been properly maintained. Prosperity had never forsaken that place. It looked just as inviting as in the days when Tottie and Elvina had done their best to quench the village thirst. The Lion was bright and red from a fresh coat of paint and varnish. It properly represented England's most flourishing industry.

We visited the green, often pictured in my mind as a great expanse of cricket field and playground, now in actuality shrunk to the dimensions of a goose pasture. How had we played cricket in such a limited field? We were little boys and did not knock the ball a mile. We wandered through the churchyard where Snobey had buried at least one generation. We viewed the tiny Methodist chapel which I had attended more than fifty years previous and where I had so greatly enjoyed the lusty singing. Nothing had changed. East Anglia does not change noticeably in fifty years and not much in one or two hundred years. How could a little boy ever have been so happy where so little of interest appeared? Happiness is a state of mind and not one of physical surroundings.

We rented a car with driver and rode from London to John O'Groats, and from there to Lands End, spending a month on the trip. It was a somewhat belated honeymoon, but we enjoyed it more than we would have done had we made the trip at the time we were married. It was in fact the most pleasurable experience in the lives of either of us. While we saw a great deal on this trip in which we covered thirty-three hundred miles, we saw but a small part of what the tourist in England will find of interest. Every town and most of the villages have features of interest. Kindness and hospitality were shown us everywhere. We met all classes of citizenry—other than royalty; they were all equally kind. I flatter myself with the thought that in many instances I was regarded as American born which, considering the brogue of East Anglia, is a long step in some direction.

The mistress of Girton College invited us to take tea with her—a charming cultured lady. As I sipped her excellent tea, I was reminded—but did not mention the experience—of the days when I made tea by boiling the leaves on board the *Eclipse*. Her cakes were most delicious, but I could not persuade myself that they tasted any better—than in my memory—did those my mother made. We accepted an invitation to dinner with the Mayor of Westminster, a fine fellow, who no doubt was mayor of that important borough for reasons of personal and exceptional fitness. We spent one day at Cambridge and one day at Rugby with some young friends. I had this opportunity of going through those two famous seats of learning but I did it in reverse, spending the first day at Cambridge and the second at Rugby.

England has played a prominent rôle in the world's history and development. Generally speaking, the British—I have never found any qualities in the Scotch and English which were not mutual—are people of fine character, and it is well to have in mind that more than fifty per cent of the white people of the United States are of British extraction. If the British do not possess the characteristics which make for honesty and general social fitness, then America is unfortunate to that extent. But their country is very much overpopulated. Its natural resources, never very great, are in the main exhausted or the product no longer in demand. Hundreds of years of prosperity, which was not equitably shared, have built up a lot of smug and self-satisfied conditions. The country now is hopelessly in debt. In the past they have been great explorers, pioneers, and traders, and as sailors they are equaled only by the Norwegians, but there are no new lands to discover and explore, no more primitive people to exploit, and if there were opportunities for further discoveries and rewards for explorations, I doubt that the present generation would be much interested.

As a boy I was fascinated by the word America. Today it apparently means nothing to the would-be adventurer other than the home of gangsters and criminals, and the place where the cinema stars live. English newspapers overplay the unattractive features of American life, and for that matter life anywhere outside of England, with the result that most young people think that their opportunities—which as a matter of fact are almost nonexistent—are just as good at home as they would be if they left their homes and associates and that glittering promise of ten shillings a week pension when they reach the age of sixty-five. This is a mistake. With at least a fifty per cent overpopulation, the young of both sexes should be persuaded to go to lands which can at least produce the food to feed them. The standard of living among the working classes, and also all other classes, is far below what it is in America. But they are strenuously opposed to any change and accept and persuade themselves that they are happy in the acceptance of conditions that the average American would find intolerable. They are encouraged to hope for the return of England's former position of supremacy in world trade. They do not realize that the "economic game" is already in the Japanese bag. They are slaves to tradition; a Chinaman could teach them nothing on that score. Their ridiculous weights and monetary systems require a daily expenditure of an enormous amount of mental effort, time, and thought which could no doubt be expended to better purpose in some other way. They insist on driving on the opposite side of the road from the people of any other country where any form of wheeled vehicle is used.

While statistics may show a rapidly declining birth rate, it so far has not become stationary. The span of life has been greatly lengthened and, with the serenity which the old-age pension—a most worthy social consideration—will produce in the minds of those who become its recipients, it will be even more extended, all of which aggravates the already overcrowded condition. Figuratively speaking, when those old people become pensioners, they will live forever. With the ten shillings weekly, they can buy some lotion for their rheumatics and spend the balance for very plain food, and if there is anything which will prolong life more than a limited amount of very plain food, it may be known to dieticians but it is not known to me.

Not much more than half of England's limited area is susceptible of profitable cultivation, and only a fractional part of Scotland has ever been made to produce anything but heather. In East Anglia sugar beets are now extensively grown, while butter and pork products, which should be produced in that district, are imported from Denmark and other continental countries. Sugar should be produced in some of the Empire's semitropic colonies. All I know, or at least most of the little I know of farming, was learned before I was thirteen, but I am sure that growing sugar beets will not maintain the fertility of the soil as would hog raising and dairying. Mr. Pilcher knew that much and he did not get up till nine in the morning, by which time most of the knowledge worth possessing had been absorbed by others. There is but small opportunity for experimenting with the subsistence farm idea for the reason that land is not available for such projects.

While the climate of England is not such as usually attracts tourists, still, if the visitor is properly advised as to the seasons, a visit, as in the case of my wife and myself, can be made very enjoyable. There is hardly a noticeable difference in the appearance of the country or in the habits of the people of East Anglia today and when I spent my happy childhood there. The same little quaint vine-covered cottages are in evidence and are generally very much admired by Americans when any of them are so fortunate as to be detoured off the regular routes to these more unfrequented counties. But these little vine-covered cottages usually have cold brick floors and no sanitary conveniences whatever. Those who spend their lives in them develop rheumatic pains before growing pains are ended.

The vibration caused by passing motor lorries is working havoc to the stone, brick and rubble, abbeys, churches, and other historic buildings. The smell of fish at both Yarmouth and Lowestoft must now be much less objectionable to "better class" tourists for the reason that the fishing industry of those two formerly important ports has faded away almost to the point of nonexistence. The trawling fishing grounds have been largely worked out. The herring, which are apparently as plentiful and delicious as ever, are not in demand. Russia, a former good customer for English herring, is now eating something else in place of that delicacy, or if we believe some reports we read, they are not eating much of anything. Germany, formerly another heavy buyer, is now without funds for the purchase of herring. The British proletariat who formerly thought that a bloater was the last word in fine living have developed a taste for Danish bacon, which of course is not nearly as good for them even if it costs less.

London is a charming place if very extensive sections of it are avoided, but to me it has always appeared as inviting a conflagration with its narrow and congested streets. Small towns in agricultural districts are usually quite charming. Industrial centers are for the most part grimy and unattractive, but industrial centers are not usually attractive in America.

There is plenty of snobbery still practiced in England, but it is not left to the nobility to display it. It is much more in evidence lower down the social line.

I have heard much criticism from American travelers of the poor quality of English coffee. I wonder if Methuselah drank coffee? Their criticism may be justified. I discovered when I was a longshoreman that though I was strong enough to carry sacks of grain for fifteen hours at a stretch, I was not strong enough to drink coffee so I am not competent to express an opinion on the lack of quality in English coffee. But you can get good tea in England, usually much better than that served in America. I know a lot about tea; I used to make it. Other travelers complain about the food. English food is fine if you work hard enough to need that kind of food. I always gain in weight when on visits to England, which indicates that whatever else may be wrong with their food, it is not lacking in sustenance.

In England you can leave your shoes in the hall when you go to bed in one of their hotels. What a joke one would play on themselves if they made that a practice in America. You can leave the door of your hotel room unlocked; in fact, in many places outside London there will be no choice in the matter as the doors have no keys. You will be served by people who know their work and who regard it as a profession, or at least as a trade, and not just a means of working their way through college—people who plan to spend the rest of their lives or at least till they can qualify for the pension—doing that same thing. It is only when they stumble, as I did, on such disturbing verse as, "In that fair region far away," that they become dissatisfied with their lot. Contentment rather than happiness is the aim and much easier of attainment.

One sight which will depress your spirits as you tour Great Britain is the large number of "monuments" which have been erected in memory of those who lost their lives in the great war, waged with people who differed from them only in the language they spoke. Many of these "monuments" are constructed of soft sandstone, which as early as 1930 was beginning to flake and show deterioration. A yew tree or a cluster of yews and a bronze plate set in a granite block and bearing the names of those who had lost their lives would have been a more permanent means of commemorating their memories, many of whom had been taken before life, which holds so much for all, had hardly begun. The erection of such frail memorials is not doing very much for the "Glory of God," which sentence appears on many of them, and it provides but a most transient record of those whose names are inscribed on the markers.

When you read about poor boys who never had a chance to get on in the world, restrain your tears until you have had time to consider each individual case. Poor boys are often happy boys, and certainly wealth is no guarantee of happiness. My happiness, up to the age of twelve, was supreme. It was not till I was old enough to make it worth while for Mr. Pilcher and others to exploit me that I knew dissatisfaction with my lot. One of the advantages of being born poor is that every step forward in ma-

(264)

terial progress—if that is the standard by which you would measure earthly rewards—is that much gained. If you are so fortunate as to be sent out into the world, ignorant and uninformed, every bit of knowledge acquired brings a thrill as an additional reward for your efforts. Had I my life to live again, I would ask for nothing more than to be born with everything before me and kind and honest parents to start me on my way. The joy of life is in the pursuit and not in the attainment.